T0062977

IF ONLY I KNEW WHERE TO FIND HIM!

*Biblical Insights for Times When
You're Wondering Where God Is*

S A M   M A S O N

Inspiring Voices®

Inspiring Voices books may be ordered through booksellers or by contacting:

Inspiring Voices
1663 Liberty Drive
Bloomington, IN 47403
www.inspiringvoices.com
1 (866) 697-5313

Cover photo by Eric Ashburn.

ISBN: 978-1-4624-1183-2 (sc)
ISBN: 978-1-4624-1184-9 (e)

Library of Congress Control Number: 2016903031

Print information available on the last page.

Inspiring Voices rev. date: 02/29/2016

TABLE OF CONTENTS

ACKNOWLEDGEMENTS

Outside of our personal relationship with God, no blessings in life exceed those provided by family and friends. I certainly have been richly endowed with precious family and friends. Once more I find myself indebted to three of these who have previously been of great help in the writing of my books. This present effort is another example of the value of their kind assistance. Their proof-reading work and reviews have helped make this book a more effective tool for communicating the truths of God's Word. Their encouragement has strengthened my conviction to move forward with its completion and publication.

Carol Dawn (Thomas) Mason is my wife, helpmate, and the love of my life. Dr. Darrell Waller is my Pastor and beloved companion in the Faith. Linda Jary is my dear friend and accomplished fellow writer. Their labor of love on behalf of my Lord, my book, and myself is truly appreciated. My thanks and yours should go out to this special trio. May God richly bless them!

INTRODUCTION

For the true believer, the Presence of God is the most precious commodity in the universe. King David, the one the Lord described as "a man after my own heart" (Acts 13:22), recognized that the most satisfying pleasure in life was to be experienced under its influence. "...You will fill me with joy in your presence" (Psalm 16:11). Those who have once tasted of the incomparable bliss that accompanies the palpable Presence of the Most High, afterward find it impossible to be fully satisfied by anything of this earth. Their longing for it endures for a lifetime.

Though intensely desired by the spiritually thirsty, the Divine Presence is often greatly misunderstood by those same seekers. Let me explain. What I've been talking about to this point is not *simply* the Presence of God, it's *specifically* what is referred to by some as the **Manifest Presence**. That means that the Presence of God is manifest, or perceptibly demonstrated, to human beings. In other words, in such times God has chosen to make people clearly aware of His Presence by one means or another. It may be exhibited by an obvious answer to one of our prayers. We could be made conscious of it through an inner spiritual sense, a powerful emotional response, or perhaps even via some supernatural display of God's power discernable in the natural realm.

This book is about those times when His Presence seems to be missing. We can see no evidence that God is actively involved in our lives. Often such periods come in the midst of difficult, even painful, trials. Prayers may appear not just to go *unanswered*, but *unheard!* That's when the confusion about God's Presence arises. No Christian is totally immune to these experiences. This sort of episode may be of relatively brief duration, lasting only days or weeks. It might even linger, however, for months or years, making our walk with the Lord an extended struggle to maintain our faith.

We may be inclined to think that the Lord is not there when His Presence is not manifest. Not so. To begin with, we must understand that one of the attributes of God is that He is everywhere at the same time. Scripture makes this truth plain in various passages. Among others it's described identically in Deuteronomy 4:39 and Joshua 2:11. Yahweh is "…God in heaven above and on the earth below." The "earth below" is, of course, the place where humans dwell, while "heaven above" refers not only to the Heaven the Bible speaks of as God's dwelling place, but to the entire universe beyond our planet.

In Psalm 139:7-10, David, inspired by the Holy Spirit, lists numerous places in the universe where he could roam and still not escape the Divine Presence. No matter where he traveled he would find God there. That's because the Lord is not restricted by space. He is in all places at once. This is called **Omnipresence**. It may not be detectable by us, and it doesn't necessarily confer any blessing from God, but it *is* the very real Presence of the Almighty.

Yet another form of God's Presence is His **Covenant Presence**. When God and men enter into covenant, He commits to be with them in a special way *at all times*. After renewing the Old Covenant between Israel and Yahweh, Moses urged the people to be strong, courageous, and not afraid, telling them that God would *always* be with them. "...He will never leave you nor forsake you" (Deuteronomy 31:6,8). In Hebrews 13:5 this same promise is reiterated for those now under the New Covenant: "... God has said, 'Never will I leave you; never will I forsake you.'" This manner of God's Presence *does* carry blessing, protection, and provision for those under His Covenant, but we're not always conscious of it.

The above types of the Presence of the Lord are all applicable this side of eternity, but there yet remains the greatest form of God's Presence. The Apostle Paul speaks of it in I Corinthians 5:6-8. "Therefore we are always confident and know that as long as we are at home in the body we are away from the Lord. We live by faith, not by sight. We are confident, I say, and would prefer to be away from the body and at home with the Lord." This is the **Fullness of His Presence**. It will surpass the glory of any divine visitation possible on this planet. We won't experience it though, until we are finally at home with Him in Heaven.

Until that eternal day, from our perspective the next best thing is that with which this book primarily deals: the aforementioned Manifest Presence of God. It's the most glorious treasure this side of Heaven. Omnipresence remains in place at all times but we're unaware of it and it doesn't necessarily offer any benefit to those outside Divine Covenant. Covenant Presence can only be lost if we deliberately break Covenant with the Lord by turning our backs on Him, yet it too usually remains indiscernible to our senses. So in most cases when it appears God has forsaken us, it's the absence of His Manifest Presence. That distinction is important to keep in mind as you read this book.

We wish we could walk always in God's Manifest Presence. Still, each of us go through times when it seems the Lord is far away and has forgotten us. As we previously pointed out, such periods often bring confusion. Discouragement, and even feelings of abandonment can develop, too. We want answers. Why are things going wrong? Why can't we hear His voice? We yearn for a return to a powerful sense of His Presence and the wonderful joy and peace it brings. These troubling periods are the times when, like Job of old, we cry out in desperation: "If only I knew where to find him!" (Job 23:3).

The Word of God has valuable insights for us. Maybe they won't include all the details we yearn to know about our own personal situations, but we'll learn that we're not alone in these kinds of circumstances. Old and New Testament saints have faced comparable trials... and have come through them in ultimate victory. So can we!

God gave youthful Joseph an extraordinary dream of leadership. Yet his own brothers sold him into slavery, where in spite of living righteously, he was falsely accused of attempted rape. As a result he unfairly languished for a long time in prison. A royal servant whom he had helped while they were behind bars together, agreed to remember him to Pharaoh when he got out, but quickly forgot Joseph. Where was the Lord and the dream He had given him?

Though Yahweh had promised the land of Canaan to the Children of Israel, they had to leave it in a time of famine and spent 400 years in abject slavery in a foreign land, wondering if God had forgotten them. As a child, Moses was supernaturally rescued from death and called by the Lord to lead Israel out of bondage and back to their promised land. Yet as a young man he found himself fleeing a death sentence, and subsequently spent 40 bewildering years as a lowly desert shepherd. That was followed by another 40 years wandering through the wilderness with a stiff-necked, complaining horde of followers. During this wilderness journey Moses sometimes felt uncertain of where God was and what He was doing.

King David, the previously cited *man after God's own heart*, felt so abandoned by the Lord on occasions that more than once in the Psalms he asked why God seemed to hide Himself. At one point David cried out in despair: "My God, my God, why have you forsaken me?" (Psalm 22:1). Even our Lord Jesus Himself shouted those very same words while hanging on the cross, when He for the first time in His life experienced the absence of His Father's Presence. In that awful moment God had to turn His back on the sins of the whole world, sacrificially borne by our substitute: the sinless Son of God, our Savior. (Matthew 27:46). I believe that was the most terrifying element of Jesus' excruciating crucifixion.

We won't be looking into the above mentioned accounts, or a number of similar ones in Scripture. We will, however, carefully examine five other prayerfully chosen relevant Bible stories. There we'll discover basic principles that can be applied to comparable experiences in our own journeys. They'll help us better deal with what's going on, in a way that will honor the Lord and in due course benefit us. Pray for God to speak to your heart as we study these real life tales from Scripture. Don't despair, my brother or sister. Our current problems can become a rugged but rewarding mountain trail, leading to a higher understanding of His ways and a richer relationship with Him!

CHAPTER 1

WHERE ARE THE ANSWERS?

Had he been introduced to us by a modern American writer, the first descriptive term used to portray him would likely have been "rich," perhaps even "filthy rich." Yes, he *was rich*, but there was nothing *filthy* about this man. The inventory of his abundant possessions a few verses into the Bible's narrative of his life confirms his vast wealth. Still, this is not how God chose to introduce "the greatest man among all the people of the East." Following his name and address, the first two adjectives the Lord used to define him were "blameless" and "upright." He then went on to declare that this mortal was "a man who fears God and shuns evil."

That those highly complimentary statements from the opening verse of the book which bears his name were not simply the perspective of the inspired writer is made clear a few verses later. Virtually identical words are found in direct quotes from the Almighty Himself in chapter 1, verse 8, and chapter 2, verse 3. God's Word leaves no doubt that this man was special in the eyes of the Lord.

SAM MASON

We're left with the compelling sense that he was a man of extraordinary character whom we should admire and emulate. These are our first impressions of the individual whose tragic story consumes more ink than any other personal ordeal recorded in all of Scripture: Job.

The 2nd and 3rd verses of chapter 1 continue the initial details of the life of the man who will soon face the darkest days of his existence. "He had seven sons and three daughters, and he owned seven thousand sheep, three thousand camels, five hundred yoke of oxen and five hundred donkeys, and had a large number of servants. He was the greatest man among all the people of the East." That his wealth was counted primarily in animals is likely a puzzle to those who live in the 21st century Western world. Such creatures are an obscure foreign currency to us. Comparing this accounting with other historical records of the general period however, leaves no doubt as to Job's financial status. He was the ancient equivalent of a billionaire!

Job's fear of God and love for his family are firmly established in verses 4 and 5. There we're told that his 10 children frequently enjoyed feasts hosted on a rotating basis by his 7 sons. We're not told the specific nature of these gatherings. Were they religious or just familial? We don't know. It would seem that the siblings enjoyed one another's company. Since Job 1:13 informs us that they were drinking wine, we're left to wonder whether the drinking may have led to drunkenness. Uncertainty over that also lingers.

In any case, Job was concerned about his children's relationship with God. In a context and cultural background that appears to be non-Jewish, he nonetheless knew and feared the one true God: Yahweh. He acted as high priest of his family. Through early morning burnt offerings he sacrificed on behalf of his offspring, Job regularly sought the Lord's forgiveness for any sins they may have committed. The world in general, and the Body of Christ in particular, could use more such concerned and proactive parents.

That this remarkably righteous person was about to suffer intensely despite his present prosperity should not totally shock us, given that his very name is considered to be derived from the Hebrew word for *affliction*. Besides, most of us understand that no one is exempt from one level or another of life's sorrows. What likely *will* surprise the first-time reader of Job are the circumstances which served as the catalyst for his distressing spiritual trial.

Beginning at verse 6 of chapter 1, the curtain is drawn back on a dramatic scene in Heaven... one to which the mortal Job was not privy. It's the sort of scene that is not at all uncommon. It has occurred repeatedly throughout the ages. The angels arrived to present themselves before the Divine Throne. The purpose of this assembly is not stated. Perhaps they were reporting on their missions, preparing to receive new orders, or both. One whom we would consider an interloper also appeared. His name is Satan, meaning *accuser*, and he was once more about to live up to that designation.

Though in His omniscience God already knew the answer, He nonetheless asked Satan where he'd been. The devil's reply reflected his routine terrestrial activities: "From roaming the earth and going back and forth in it." Centuries later the Apostle Peter warns believers of Satan's intentions during such journeys. "Your enemy the devil prowls around like a roaring lion looking for someone to devour" (I Peter 5:8).

The next words uttered by God would soon initiate the lighting of a fuse to an explosive set of events that would tear apart Job's comfortable world and leave devastation in its wake. Those words were not, however, words of judgment, but of praise. The Creator was bragging on His servant! "Have you considered my servant Job? There is no one on earth like him; he is blameless and upright, a man who fears God and shuns evil" (Job 1:8).

Satan's response was not admiration, but accusation. This is who the devil is and what he does. A similar picture is presented in Zechariah 3:1, where we see "...Joshua the high priest standing before the angel of the LORD, and Satan standing at his right side to accuse him." The last book of the Bible reveals the broad scope of the enemy's attack. He's not just after a Job here and a Joshua there. "For the accuser of our brothers, who accuses them before our God day and night, has been hurled down" (Revelation 12:10). Thank God, the devil's malicious schemes will one day come to an end, but for now, we must be aware of them. *All* of the Heavenly Father's blood-bought children have a target on their back.

Job's righteous lifestyle had allowed God's goodness to flow freely, but Satan argued the reverse. "Does Job fear God for nothing?", he inquired. "Have you not put a hedge around him and his household and everything he has? You have blessed the work of his hands, so that his flocks and herds are spread throughout the land" (1:9,10). Rather than Job enjoying divine blessings as a result of honoring God, the devil insisted that Job only honored God because the Lord had blessed him. The accuser concluded his diatribe by declaring of Job: "…stretch out your hand and strike everything he has, and he will surely curse you to your face" (1:11). Satan's negative assessment of God's servant was proffered, and the challenge for Job and His God to prove him wrong had been issued.

The One who fully knows every human heart was confident of Job's godly character. He granted the enemy permission to do what he does so efficiently: to suck the fullness of life from humanity, entering every situation he can to "steal and kill and destroy" (John 10:10). Yahweh did draw a line, however. "…Everything he has is in your hands, but on the man himself do not lay a finger" (1:12). With that, the devil left to do his dirty work. The man whom God had greatly blessed and openly defined in glowing terms was about to be blindsided.

The suddenness and reach of Satan's attack were stunning. In a single day, through overlapping reports, Job discovered that his private world had been destroyed! First he was told that every one of his oxen and donkeys had been stolen, and all but one of his servants attending them had been put to the sword. On the heels of that came the account of fire falling from the sky, burning up his sheep and shepherds, sparing only the one who lived to tell that story. Next came the news that Job's camels had been carried off and the nearby servants, save one, had been slain. The final blow must have dropped poor Job to the canvas. A mighty wind had collapsed the house where his children had been feasting and a single surviving servant arrived to deliver the demoralizing details of their deaths.

The devil had enlisted men and nature to come against Job. It's no different today. The enemy of our souls has numerous devious weapons at his disposal. Included

5

among them are wayward human beings and the forces of nature. We may think that people are basically good and that earth's atmosphere is the exclusive domain of God, but we must remember that Satan is "...the ruler of the kingdom of the air, the spirit who is now at work in those who are disobedient" (Ephesians 2:2). The means he sometimes uses to assault God's people may shock us, but it shouldn't. Such naiveté will only add to our emotional trauma.

By human standards Job's initial response to his overwhelming losses is both predictable and unexpected. In keeping with the traditions of his era he tore his robe and shaved his head as an expression of intense grief. Job then fell to the ground in what would normally be interpreted as a symbol of his deep sorrow. But in this case his prostration seemed rather to be in worship. The words that poured from Job's heart through his lips revealed incredible trust in God. "Naked I came from my mother's womb, and naked I will depart. The LORD gave and the LORD has taken away; may the name of the LORD be praised" (1:21). The sacred record of this part of the story ends with a proclamation of Job's unquestioned piety. "In all this, Job did not sin by charging God with wrongdoing" (1:22).

The accuser had insisted that Job only feared God for the material blessings he gained as a result. Job's reaction to the destruction of his once impressive estate proved Satan wrong. God's servant honored the Most High not for what he could get from Him, but for Who He was. Job had maintained his righteous integrity in the wake of unimaginable loss.

What about us? Do we serve God for His blessings, or do we give Him His rightful place as Sovereign of our lives simply because He deserves it? Would our grief in time of such bereavement yield to worship of the God who allowed such tragedy to strike us? Or would we complain bitterly, shake our fist angrily at the Almighty, and perhaps even give up in despair? Lord, help us to trust You fully and follow you closely through every tribulation of life.

At this point in the story some may ask: "What about those who suffered with Job in Satan's attack... the sheep who died, Job's children and servants whose earthly lives were snuffed out? And what of the families of those who were lost in these far-reaching disasters? Was God content to allow them to be used merely as pawns in Job's test?" The book of Job is focused on its central character and doesn't deal with these questions about the others. For that reason I won't deal in depth with them here either. That's not to say that these questions are not legitimate concerns, however. So let me very briefly address the issue and then we'll move on.

Although the account of Job's trial is silent on these specific matters, Scripture elsewhere supplies enough general information about the Lord's nature to make it plain that He's never callous toward *any* life. In the Old Testament He's depicted as the Creator who provides for His creatures and wants humans to do the same. Proverbs 12:10 says "A righteous man cares for the needs of his animal..." In the New Testament the Lord is seen as moved by the plight of a single bird. "Are not five sparrows sold for two pennies? Yet not one of them is forgotten by God" (Luke 12:6). This fact is used as a springboard to proclaim His compassion for every person on earth.

"Indeed, the very hairs of your head are all numbered. Don't be afraid; you are worth more than many sparrows" (Luke 12:7). No, the other victims of Job's calamities were not just pawns, the Lord loved them all.

Now back to the thrust of the book of Job. Having passed the test by trusting God and not charging Him with wrongdoing in the aftermath of a horrendous host of losses, the object of the devil's finger pointing is once again the subject of conversation in the Throne Room. The opening verse of chapter 2 introduces the scene this way: "On another day the angels came to present themselves before the LORD, and Satan also came with them to present himself before him."

The dialogue during this second encounter began the same as the first. The Almighty asked Satan from where he had come. Then following the devil's answer, God repeated His original positive assessment of Job. He followed it up with a statement which essentially challenged the devil to admit defeat. "And he still maintains his integrity, though you incited me against him to ruin him without any reason" (2:3).

Satan apparently remained unconvinced of Job's integrity... or is it rather that he remained convinced of his evil power to convert humanity to his own unjust rebellion against the Almighty. Lucifer is nothing if not arrogant! "'Skin for skin!' Satan replied. 'A man will give all he has for his own life. But stretch out your hand and strike his flesh and bones, and he will surely curse you to your face'" (2:4,5). Job would later express unshakeable trust in God, contradicting the enemy's claim of "skin for skin." But in that moment He was completely unaware of the debate raging in Heaven over his character.

Standing by His optimistic appraisal of Job's godly character, Yahweh basically told the devil "Go for it." Once more, however, God drew the line, this time telling Satan he must spare Job's life. With that, the enemy departed God's Heavenly Kingdom and returned to his own territory on earth. The bell for the start of round 2 was about to ring.

As with the previous calamities which befell Job, it must be noted that this next one was manufactured by the devil, not God. Job 2:7 plainly states: "So Satan went out from the presence of the LORD and afflicted Job with painful sores from the soles of his feet to the top of his head." Yahweh had allowed all of the terrible troubles to descend upon His servant, but He had not been the source of them. We must always remember that our enemy is not the Lord. Our enemy is "the accuser of our brothers:" Satan (Revelation 12:10).

According to some Bible scholars this scene likely finds Job sitting "among the ashes" of the town dump. Early mourners in this part of the world often went to such a place for a time to express their intense grief. It was this cheerless venue into which the devil entered and covered Job's body with "painful sores" from head to foot. I, as with most believers, have experienced periods of multiplied difficulties. Still, I can hardly imagine what it must have been like for this upright man who had already suffered incredible losses to now find himself in intense, unrelenting physical pain on top of it all. Yet Job was about to absorb still another staggering blow.

The only glimpse of Job's wife we're afforded in this entire lengthy account is not a complimentary one. While her husband sought to honor God in the midst of one of recorded history's most distressing set of circumstances, she arrived at the dunghill to present him with a remarkably disturbing question. "Are you still holding on to your integrity?" Her tone appeared to imply the foolish futility of such stubborn adherence to godly standards. She followed up her question with an astounding piece of advice for her husband. "Curse God and die!"

In some ways I see this incident as the lowest moment in Job's experience up to this point. The dearest person on earth... the love of his life... had just advised him that his efforts to walk uprightly before God and men had been a waste! She urged him to throw in the towel in the most spiteful way. "Curse God and die!" Could anything in life be as painful as your spouse assessing the entire course of your life as a mistake... then urging your foot toward the proverbial bucket?

In spite of this excruciating personal rejection, Job stood his ground. He gripped his integrity more strongly than ever and rebuked his wife's perspective. "You are talking like a foolish woman. Shall we accept good from God, and not trouble?" (2:10). In the wake of such a compelling statement Scripture goes on to declare that "In all this, Job did not sin in what he said."

It's at this low point in his sufferings that my admiration for Job rises to a peak. Here is a man who had faced down some of the most potent weapons the enemy could throw at him, and had refused to yield to the temptation to renounce his faith! He remained "more than a conqueror" (Romans 8:37), not surrendering his tongue to sinful impulses. Though he never would curse God as Satan had originally asserted, Job would eventually entertain thoughts and utter words he'd regret. In this current valley of misery, however, the man was the model of a faithful servant of the Lord.

The news of Job's troubles had traveling feet, and reached the ears of three friends: Eliphaz the Temanite, Bildad the Shuhite, and Zophar the Naamathite. They made plans to leave their homes, meet at a prearranged location, then slip to their friend's side to sympathize with him. Though centuries later the disparaging expression "Job's comforters" would arise from their eventually judgmental words, there's no reason to doubt their early sincere concern for their friend.

The Biblical description of their initial reaction to Job's appearance exhibits the kind of deep compassion we might expect from true friends. "When they saw him from a distance, they could hardly recognize him; they began to weep aloud, and they tore their robes and sprinkled dust on their heads. Then they sat on the ground with him for seven days and seven nights. No one said a word to him, because they saw how great his suffering was" (2:12,13).

Though the weeklong silence of Job's friends may have been in keeping with some appropriate ancient tradition, I think personally I would have found it unsettling rather than comforting. Maybe, just maybe, Job had a similar reaction. Could it be that the intense hush contributed to the somber mental machinations which culminated in Job's unforeseen diatribe a week later? The misery of unanswered questions began to poke through the fortress walls of his righteous philosophy of life. In a relatively short span of time he would go from virtuous acceptance of personal tragedies, to distraught rejection of his very existence.

Look back at the Scriptural statement that describes Job's pious response to his wife's unkind words just a few verses earlier. "In all this Job did not sin *in what he said.*" Those last four words hint that something awry may have been stirring deep within Job's soul. God's servant did not sin "in what he said." How powerful is human speech? Proverbs 18:21 tells us "The tongue has the power of life and death…" Wow! James 3:2 further instructs us that "… if anyone is never at fault in what he says, he is a perfect man, able to keep his whole body in check."

Thoughts repeatedly entertained, however, will eventually slide off our tongues. In due course that's what happened to Job. However horrific a crisis might come our way, it may not be able to quickly topple the godly trust of the more stalwart believers. Ah, but the *persistence* of a severe ongoing trial can sometimes wear down even such pillars of the faith. The human mind then is inclined to descend into dark caverns of doubt.

Satan had claimed that if his fortunes turned, Job would curse *God.* Thankfully, that prediction never came to pass, but this blameless and upright man did come uncomfortably close to fulfilling that wicked prophecy. He cursed *the day of his birth.* The Bible indicates that life is under God's juristiction and ought not to be arbitrarily rejected or interrupted by mere men. David, Isaiah, and Jeremiah all proclaimed that the Lord knew them and had plans for their lives before they were born. David further spoke with assurance that all the moments of his life were in the hands of God (Psalm 31:15). Job's rejection of his own birth was in a sense a rejection of God's sovereignty.

His rant in chapter 3 reeks of bitterness. Great suffering can cause us to lose our sense of purpose in life. I've personally witnessed this phenomenon even in the lives of some of the Lord's finest saints. Over time Job reached the point where he despised his very life. He felt it would have been better if he'd never been born. Have you ever been there? Are you there now? If you maintain your confidence in God, like Job you'll eventually rediscover God's goodness.

For the next 35 chapters there is not a single thought or word coming directly from the Almighty Himself. More than 80% of the book of Job is devoted to the ongoing dialogue among Job, his three friends, and a somewhat mysterious fifth person named Elihu. Undoubtedly truths about Yahweh are uttered by this quintet, but they're mingled with misguided human musings about the Creator. The bulk of the inspired record is a revelation of what these men believe about God and men.

The debate which follows Job's opening discourse began in civil enough fashion. As the protracted conversations wore on though, the niceties wore down. Sympathy and respect disintegrated into sarcasm and ridicule. Job and his companions spoke with a self-confident sense of authority while criticizing one another and mixing truth with error. I'm reminded of Proverbs 10:19: "When words are many, sin is not absent..." This is not to infer that any of these men were wicked... just characteristically flawed human beings. Like many believers of all eras, they thought they knew more about God, themselves, and one another, than was actually the case.

My objective in writing about Job's story does not include creating a detailed critique of these middle chapters of the book. Yet I do want to glean some valuable insights, especially from Job's discourses. Many of the man's notions about God and life may be ours as well. So let's see what we might learn from them.

First, let me repeat what I said about the words spoken by all five of these men. It applies, of course, to Job's statements, too. *They're a mixture of truth and error.* Like every other believer, Job did not possess all knowledge. Like the rest of us, his faith was not perfect. He vacillated between spiritual fact and fiction, trust and uncertainty. On the one hand Job accused the Lord of wronging him (19:6,7). Yet in that same passage he expressed supreme confidence that his Redeemer lived and that he'd someday see Him (19:25-27). Job's wavering back and forth between secure confidence in, and nagging questions about God's care of His children, is a pattern of thought also seen throughout the candid writings of the psalmists. Don't despair when you battle doubts yourself, my brother or sister. Cling to your hope in God in the midst of the battles. He will ultimately honor your imperfect human trust.

In his ongoing ruminations, Job was guilty of trying to bring God down to his own level. He wanted to argue his case before His Maker. Those desires presuppose two things: 1) We are wise enough to fully understand the Lord and His ways, and 2) we can justify ourselves and argue our way into His blessings. Such foolishness reminds me of a prudent piece of advice I heard many years ago: "Your arms are too short to box with God!" We're not as smart as we think, and we're totally dependent on the Lord's mercy.

Often a little spiritual knowledge goes quickly to our heads. Seek to know Him better every day, friend. Study

His Word, seek His Face in prayer, sit under sound Bible teaching… but *never* presume that you know all there is to know about God and how He works! You'll not arrive at that destination this side of eternity. In speaking of our inability to forecast what the Lord might do, author and speaker Graham Cooke once put it this way: "There's absolutely no security for you in what God is doing. There's only security in Who He is… He is consistent, but He's also unpredictable. You always know where you are with God, but you seldom know what He's going to do next." I might sum it up like this: His mercy endures forever, but His ways are always higher than our ways.

There's a part of us that would like to remake God in our own image, in some sense to "mortalize" Him in an effort to make Him more understandable. How silly! The Lord addressed the folly of such an attitude when He rebuked His children in Psalm 50:21: "…you thought I was altogether one like you." The doxology found in Romans 11:33-36 seeks to raise our thinking on this matter. "Oh, the depth of the riches of the wisdom and knowledge of God! How unsearchable his judgments, and his paths beyond tracing out! Who has known the mind of the Lord? Or who has been his counselor? Who has ever given to God, that God should repay him? For from him and through him and to him are all things. To him be the glory forever! Amen."

While the Bible, as God's Word, communicates His ways to us as effectively as earthly language can, remember it too has its limits. At the conclusion of his inspired account of the Gospel of Christ, the Apostle John alluded to one such limit. "Jesus did many other things as well. If every one of them were written down, I suppose that even the whole world would not have room for the books that would be written" (John 21:25). Scripture is not a box which completely defines the Lord and fully circumscribes every detail of His activities. It's simply an earthly portal to an incomplete understanding of Who He is and how He works... a finite glimpse into His ineffable infinite nature.

I've never forgotten how one of our instructors in Bible school reconciled the apparent contradiction of the fact that a miracle often requires God to break one of His own natural laws. "God does not obey the laws," he explained, "the laws obey God." That simple revelation can help us deal with the reality that the Lord doesn't always fit into the constraints of our finite conceptions of Him. Job needed to deal with that very issue. Despite his current confusion, God was still on the throne. Unknown happenings in the heavens had impacted his life.

Job was deeply troubled and wanted some answers from God. In one way or another, throughout his recorded speeches, Job asked "Why?" He had developed some of his own predetermined answers, yet he desperately wanted to hear clearly from God. Sound familiar? Chances are you've been there. If not yet, you probably will be someday.

So many questions flooded his soul. Most rolled off his lips in the course of time. Why had God shown him no mercy? (7:21). Why had the Lord abandoned him? (13:24). Why did ungodly people prosper while Job suffered great loss? (24:12). Most importantly he wondered where God was (23:3,8,9). Though Job longed to see the Lord (19:25-27) and yearned for His Presence and intimate friendship (19:27, 29:4), through all those dark days Job's ears never warmed to the assuring voice of God. Yahweh's silence was beyond frustrating, it was painful! Where were the answers?

When the answers he sought were not forthcoming, Job lamented the fact that the Lord seemed nowhere to be found. He wanted to personally present his case to God, to prove his innocence. He bemoaned the perceived lack of fairness in his situation. Job 32:1 informs us that "he was righteous in his own eyes." He intended to prove his righteousness in a private appearance before heaven's judicial bench. Job mistakenly thought that his native intelligence was sufficient to win an argument with God.

Job's severe trial had exposed shortcomings in his walk with God, but they did not negate his Creator's original assessment of him as a man who "fears God and shuns evil." Even the most righteous among us are still flawed human beings. Job was a *good* man who was about to discover that he could stand to become a *better* one. His request to appear before the Lord was about to be granted, but the nature and end result of that confrontation were not to be what he had expected.

As the final debater of the middle chapters of the book (the mysterious young man named Elihu) came to the close of his thoughts about God, Job, and Job's three friends, he referred to an approaching storm as an example of God's incomparable authority. Suddenly Yahweh's own voice thundered out of that very storm. Though we might wish Him to use a less stressful means of communication, God often speaks through the storms of life. All present on this occasion must have trembled at the sharp turn of events, but the divine utterances that followed were aimed at Job alone. The opening question from the Almighty must have rocked him to the core! "Who is this that darkens my counsel with words without knowledge?" (38:2).

Job had sought an audience with the Judge of the Whole Earth in order to pursue answers to his own questions. Now the tables were turned. The Lord demanded: "Brace yourself like a man; I will question you, and you will answer me." (38:3). What follows is a series of queries which left Job in stupefied silence. The questions must have seemed endless to this mere moral. "Where were you when I laid the earth's foundations?" (38:4). "Have you comprehended the vast expanses of the earth?" (38:18). "Can you bind the beautiful Pleiades?" (38:31).

The Almighty's queries went unanswered. So did Job's. Most significantly, the overall question of "why" all these terrible events took place seems never to have been resolved. As readers, the curtains of heaven had been drawn back for us in the opening chapter. We witnessed Satan's accusations against Job, and God's confidence in his righteous servant. Job, however, was not privy to that scene. And there's no indication in Scripture that the Lord *ever* revealed "why" to the man... even after his trials were over. Some questions will remain open-ended for the duration of this earthly life.

In the midst of the divine verbal barrage, Job meekly admitted: "I am unworthy how can I reply to you? I put my hand over my mouth. I spoke once, but I have no answer — twice, but I will say no more" (40:4,5). Yet the divine questioning continued. Job's acceptance of his human limitations had to come to the point where any semblance of self-reliance was eradicated. In the end, God's servant was brought to his knees as a greater man than he had been… a much more humble child of His Heavenly Father. An internal transformation had taken place. The final recorded words of Job in the tale of his great sufferings were: "Therefore I despise myself and repent in dust and ashes" (42:6). True to the Lord's expressed confidence in him, he had never cursed God, but he had indulged in self-righteousness.

The epilogue demonstrates Yahweh's unrelenting love and blessings for this saint who had emerged from a period of anguish as an even more faithful servant of God than before. I don't know of anyone who enjoys suffering. Personally, I hate suffering. But when it comes I embrace it and ask the Lord to use it to make me more like Jesus. God never declares that our lives will be free from pain. He does, however, pledge that He will bring good from that pain. Romans 5:3,4 is only one of a number of Scriptures setting forth this principle: "…but we rejoice in our sufferings, because we know that suffering produces perseverance; perseverance, character; and character, hope."

After Job's repentance, God commended him, but chided his three friends. "I am angry with you… because you have not spoken of me what was right, as my servant Job has" (42:7). At first this divine appraisal is a bit confusing. Hadn't Yahweh just rebuked Job for his contentious attitude and words? Yes, but His servant had been penitent and admitted: "Surely I spoke of things I did not understand, things too wonderful for me to know" (42:3). Eliphaz, Bildad, and Zophar apparently did not follow suit. All had spoken with a far greater feeling of authority than any human actually possesses, but only Job had confessed his error and arrogance.

The Lord established a means of restoration for Job's three friends. They were commanded to go to Job and sacrifice burnt offerings, then he would pray for them. They obeyed, Job prayed, and God accepted Job's prayer. Has someone been unkind and critical toward you? Pray for them... not for God to strike them dead either! Pray for them to be blessed!

It was in the wake of Job's prayers for those who had harshly judged him that he himself was restored to the realm of divine blessing. "After Job had prayed for his friends, the LORD made him prosperous again and gave him twice as much as he had before" (42:10). From that moment on the goodness of God flowed back into his life. His brothers, sisters, friends, and neighbors arrived to feast with him in his house... not at the town dump where he had previously mourned! They comforted him and offered him gifts. The Lord doubled his wealth and gave him seven sons and three daughters. In fact, the Bible says of his daughters that they were the most beautiful in all the land! (42:15).

The book closes with this glowing report: "After this, Job lived a hundred and forty years; he saw his children and their children to the fourth generation. And so he died, old and full of years" (42:16,17). Happy endings await those who faithfully persevere through agonizing trials. Such endings may occur in this life or the life to come, but they *will* take place. It was not only willingness to hold on to his confidence in God, but willingness to repent and grow which brought Job's test to its cheerful conclusion.

Bible teacher and author, Major W. Ian Thomas, once reminded his readers that the deepest work of repentance takes place not *at* conversion, but *after* conversion. If a man declared by God to be "blameless and upright" still had room for improvement, what about the rest of us? We surely have sins and shortcomings to deal with and plenty of need to learn and mature in the faith. What major lessons can we draw from the story of Job? We've already touched on some of those truths. Let's review and expand a little.

Lesson 1: Life's devastating events may have nothing to do with bad behavior on our part. The misconception about an undeniable connection between personal sin and personal suffering was the model largely argued by Job's friends. They insisted that he must have done something wrong. But the genesis of Job's trial was not God's displeasure with him. It was the Almighty's confidence that the man's righteous demeanor was not based on his prosperous circumstances, but his fear of God. Yahweh was certain that Job's righteousness by faith would stand the test. *Never* assume yours or anyone else's distress must be the consequence of sin. The Lord may simply be demonstrating your godly character in the midst of misfortune.

Lesson 2: Satan is the enemy, not God. All suffering entered this world as a result of the devil's interference. The Creator never designed life to include misery. Job's tragic experiences were devised in the pits of Hell, not the halls of Heaven. Satan is the "accuser of the brothers:" our adversary. The Lord is on our side, our advocate. God may allow the enemy's attacks, but He does not create them. God is a good God! Don't blame Him for the bad things that come your way.

Lesson 3: Friendship can be amazingly fickle... even *Christian* friendship! Most Christians who've spoken with me about hurtful experiences have been hurt by *fellow believers,* and the closer the relationships, the deeper the wounds. It's a sad commentary on the carnal immaturity of many who claim the name of Christ. The Bible teaches us to "...do good to all people, especially to those who belong to the family of believers" (Galatians 6:10). It also tells us to function in love. "Love is patient, love is kind. It does not envy, it does not boast, it is not proud. It is not rude, it is not self-seeking, it is not easily angered, it keeps no record of wrongs" (I Corinthians 13:4,5). That speaks to both the offender and the offended.

Lesson 4: None of us is perfect this side of heaven. Even the most godly among us can slip into ungodly attitudes and actions when trials press hard upon us. Suffering can make us *bitter* or *better.* It depends on how we react. Like Job, we may come across both the bitter and better sides of our nature during painful experiences. At times he proclaimed his own righteousness and accused God of treating him unfairly, while in other moments he exalted the Lord and expressed implicit trust in Him. In the end, when Yahweh spoke out of the storm, Job let go of his pride and bitterness. He humbled himself in repentance and became a better person for it. May we all seek to walk through our troubles in humility and trust, allowing the Lord to develop in us more godly character than before.

Lesson 5: The Master rewards those who remain faithful when the winds of adversity attempt to blow us off course. Greater blessings can emerge from the storms that we can imagine, but it takes trust and perseverance. It also requires doing what is *right* while circumstances go *wrong* and those around us treat us *wrongfully.* Yes,

Job complained, but he also determined to maintain his integrity. "...as long as I have life within me, the breath of God in my nostrils, my lips will not speak wickedness, and my tongue will utter no deceit" (27:3,4). It's significant to note that it was *after* Job prayed for his judgmental friends that "...the LORD made him prosperous again..." (42:10). Our blessings may arrive in this life, or not until eternity, but if we stay true to God they *will* come.

Lesson 6: There will always be things beyond our understanding while in these mortal bodies. We might want answers to all our questions, but it won't happen here. Our minds don't have the capacity to grasp all there is of God and His ways. That's where trust must come to the forefront. At the close of the book there still remained so many unanswered questions. How long did this trial last? Did the Lord ever tell Job how the whole thing started? Who was the enigmatic Elihu, when did he arrive on the scene, and why is his behavior not addressed at the conclusion as was that of Job and his three friends? It's as if God is saying: "I'm pulling back the curtain a little to provide a glimpse of my ways... just enough to give you reason to fear and trust me more when the curtain is closed."

I'm reminded of the words of a song by singer/songwriter Babbie Mason: "So when you don't understand, when don't see his plan, when you can't trace His hand, trust His heart." These lyrics point to the distinction between *faith* and *trust*. These two Scriptural words are intimately acquainted, yet definitely different. I don't intend to deal with this distinction in depth here, but it's pertinent enough to the things we can learn from Job's ordeal that I do want to take some space to at least briefly explain it.

In Galatians 3:23, the Apostle Paul spoke to the churches of that region about how faith "should be revealed." This verse hints at the vital connection between *faith* and *revelation*. *Faith* is based on knowledge that is directly *revealed* to each of us as individuals. It may come through a Bible passage quickened, or made alive, to us by the Holy Spirit. It might be imparted by the still small voice of God within. The bottom line is that the Lord gives us a definite word about what He is going to do. On those occasions, this thing called faith arises in our hearts and we expect God to act exactly as He said He would.

A fine example of this is provided in II Kings chapter 5. Naaman, the God-fearing commander of the Syrian army, sought healing of his leprosy from the God of Israel. He was advised by a young Jewish servant girl to seek out the prophet Elisha. Naaman thought the man of God would wave his hand over him and cure his disease. Instead, Yahweh spoke through His prophet and said: "Go wash yourself seven times in the Jordan, and your flesh will be restored and you will be cleansed" (II Kings 5:10). It took a little time, but Naaman ultimately accepted God's specific word to him. His act of faith resulted in complete healing in fulfillment of the supernatural knowledge revealed to him.

Trust, on the other hand, is for those times when the Lord hasn't shown us specifically what He's doing or is going to do. When we have no clear word from His lips, we must maintain our clear convictions about His nature. God is a good God... a loving God... a righteous God... an all-powerful God! *Trust* is the equivalent of the Biblical concept of *hope*. It may not know what's going on, or precisely what the Almighty plans to do, but it expects good from His hand. Trust reaches beyond our ignorance of His exact strategy for dealing with current circumstances, to believe that "...in all things God works for the good of those who love him..." (Romans 8:28). Job's finite mind may have been rattled by events beyond his understanding, but he kept returning to his trust in the Lord. In times of trouble, we too must cling to our trust in Him.

Faith focuses more on the *promise* of God. Trust focuses more on His *Person*. Faith believes that He's a *God of His Word*, that He'll do exactly what He's personally told us He'll do. Trust believes He's a *good God*, that whatever He does will be consistent with that divine character.

The account of Job's epic story doesn't provide all the information we may crave, but it does give us beneficial food for thought. The insights we gain can help us better navigate the treacherous trails which inevitably stretch before us as we pass through this earthly existence. May God help us to learn and live the lessons He's graciously provided. Remember, even when there's no perceivable indication of His Presence, He's always here with those of us who are under His covenant. As with Job, the Lord will work behind the scenes in our lives. He may allow trouble to invade, but He'll always draw the line on how far the enemy of our souls can go. If we refuse to surrender our trust in our Heavenly Father to our doubts, we'll come out of the valley of suffering richer than we entered it!

CHAPTER 2

GUARD YOUR EYES

Maybe you've seen some of the strongman competitions on television over the years. They feature hulking, muscular men who do amazing things like pulling trucks, flipping cars, and tossing huge, heavy kegs through the air. Witnessing their success at these events can transform your normally closed mouth into a gaping cavern. I confess, watching them appeals to my male psyche. I'd like to possess that kind of impressive might. Scripture, however, records the story of a man whose actual feats of strength would leave modern day strongmen gasping for air in utter defeat! This Biblical warrior battled Israel's arch enemies for two decades, pummeling them with his divinely endowed brute force.

Many of us who've read or heard of Samson's exploits probably picture him as an Arnold Swartzenegger type, rippling with massive muscles. My father, a longtime student of God's Word, had a different image in mind. He was convinced that Samson had just an average build. He believed the man's great strength was strictly supernatural, functioning only when the anointing of the Spirit of God fell upon him. Such a pattern would cause his enemies and countrymen to be even more astounded at what he accomplished, recognizing the hand of Yahweh at work. I've come to agree with my dad's viewpoint. I believe Samson's physique was probably rather ordinary.

But we're getting ahead of ourselves. The tale of Israel's strongman is told in the book of Judges. Judges chronicles the sporadic leadership of the fledgling Jewish homeland. God had brought His people out of slavery in Egypt under the guidance of His servant Moses. After Moses death, his protégé Joshua led them into their inheritance in the land the Lord had promised to them: Canaan. When Joshua and all those who had experienced God's miraculous interventions passed, the next generation of Jews began to turn away from the God of their fathers. They fell into idolatry, serving the false gods of the pagan Canaanites they'd failed to fully drive out of the land.

During this period of several centuries, a disturbing spiritual pattern emerged. God's children would ignore His Word and do evil. They'd consequently suffer oppression at the hands of their enemies. Then, usually as a result of their desperate cries for help to the Almighty, godly leaders would be raised up to lead them back to the Lord and to victory over the oppressors. In between these episodes of spiritual repentance and military victories, "everyone did as he saw fit" (Judges 17:6, 21:25). This was a condition God had warned against in advance through the lips of Moses. "You are not to do as we do here today, everyone as he sees fit..." (Deuteronomy 12:8).

The book of *Judges* gives us the history of Israel's *judges*. These judges did not serve in a court system as we might expect based on our use of the English word. Although these judges may have occasionally rendered legal decisions in disputes among God's children, that was not their primary responsibility. The Hebrew word for judge used in this context reaches beyond such a narrow definition. It might better be understood simply by the word *leader*. They were to call the nation back to Yahweh, and empowered by Him, deliver them from their tormentors. That was their primary function as established in chapter 2, verse 18. "Whenever the LORD raised up a judge for them, he was with the judge and saved them out of the hands of their enemies as long as the judge lived..." Unlike in a kingly dynasty, such leadership roles were not passed on to their offspring. Individual judges were called by God to lead Israel just for a season.

Chapter 13 begins by informing us that Israel had once again turned away from the Law of God. It then introduces the account of the last and most famous leader in the book, though we don't read his name until the final verses of the chapter. Why? Because his commission began before he was born and given a name... even before he was conceived. You see, divine callings aren't launched from earth, they descend from heaven. They don't emerge from the time constricted minds of men, they're born in the eternal heart of God.

The message of Yahweh's plan to begin delivering His people from the cruel domination of the Philistines was first conveyed to an obscure childless woman. We aren't even told her name, but God knew it! Celebrity is not the mark of divine approval. People may look to external and public things, but the Lord looks to the heart. Some of his finest servants labor in the shadows. We're told that this handmaiden of God was the wife of a man from the Jewish tribe of Dan. His name was Manoah. We know little of the background of the pair. What is clear is that they were about to become channels of the Lord's intervention on behalf of the entire nation, and God never makes these decisions randomly.

The "Angel of the Lord" was the envoy who brought word of God's plan to Manoah's wife. This was no run-of-the-mill messenger boy. The Angel of the Lord (or more precisely: "the Angel of Yahweh") is generally considered by Bible scholars to be the Son of God… Divinity in a heavenly body! That's why Manoah later feared they would die. He lamented to his wife "We are doomed to die! We have seen God!" (13:22) The magnitude of the announcement made to this couple was so great that the Lord Himself descended to the earth to declare it to them.

The mother-to-be was alone when she originally met the impressive stranger. His first word to her was a simple and encouraging one. "You are sterile and childless, but you are going to conceive and have a son" (13:3). Her heart must have soared at this promise! Deep within every woman is an instinctive desire to be a mother. It may be suppressed by fear, the misguided ideology of prevailing culture, or through other means, but it's undeniably inherent in the female persona. This discouraged wife was about to experience the miraculous touch of God. She was going to be a mother after all!

The next piece of information from the Angel was not so simple. It would require special consecration on the part of the mother, and an even greater level of consecration from the son. This boy was to be a Nazarite from his birth until his death. In this regard he would be unique in the annals of Bible history. Although one or two others *may possibly* have been Nazarites for their entire lives, we're unsure in their cases because it's not clearly stated. This leader of Israel would stand alone in that respect.

The Nazarite vow was explained by the Lord to Moses in Numbers chapter 6. It's introduced as an *option* for God's people. "If a man or a woman wants to make a special vow, a vow of separation to the LORD as a Nazarite..." (verse 2). It was also expected to be of a circumscribed duration. "Now this is the law for the Nazarite when the period of his separation is over..." (verse 5). That's why the calling of this unborn child was so unique. The choice was not his, it was God's. Plus, his consecration had no earthly time limit. It was to be for his entire life.

Some might consider such a condition to be an *unfair imposition*. Those who've come to know and love the Almighty, however, rightly perceive it as an *honor*. Israel's tribe of Levi understood this principle. Every other tribe received a portion of the Promised Land to call their own. Not so, the Levites. God made that decision for them. They had an exclusive ministry. Their responsibilities included carrying the hallowed Ark of the Covenant, serving in the very Presence of Yahweh, and pronouncing blessings upon their brethren in His Name. Deuteronomy 10:9 proclaims "That is why the Levites have no share or inheritance among their brothers; the LORD is their inheritance..." Those called by their Maker to a deeper level of consecration to Him possess a richer inheritance than anything this planet could ever provide. The Lord Himself is their inheritance!

The term "Nazarite" is derived from a Hebrew word meaning "to set apart." Although all Jews were God's people, and therefore in some sense "set apart" unto Him, Nazarites drew even closer to the Lord through their deeper level of commitment. As the mother of a child who was to be a Nazarite from birth, Manoah's wife had to adhere to some requirements herself during her pregnancy. She was commanded: "drink no wine or other fermented drink... and... do not eat anything unclean..." She was additionally told that after his birth "No razor may be used on his head" (13:5). The full law of the Nazarite vow is set forth in the previously cited Numbers chapter 6. The part that would give this judge his distinct appearance, however, would be the hair that was never to be cut. This was the foremost *mark* of his exceptional consecration to God.

Manoah's wife went to her husband and recounted her supernatural rendezvous. Unsure at that time just who the messenger was, she referred to him as "a man of God," yet noted that "He looked like an angel of God, very awesome" (13:6). After the astounding announcement this emissary had carried was passed on to her husband, Manoah wanted more information. Maybe he had feelings of inadequacy. He prayed for a reappearance of "the man of God," begging for instructions on how to properly rear this exceptional child.

God answered Manoah's prayer for the messenger to return. The Angel of the Lord appeared once more to his wife. She hurried to tell her husband, who wasn't with her at the time. Arriving at the scene, Manoah verified that this person was the same one who had previously talked to his wife. Then he asked: "When your words are fulfilled, what is to be the rule for the boy's life and work?" (13:12). Interestingly, the Angel didn't exactly answer Manoah's question. Instead, he reiterated the restrictions that he had already given to the mother-to-be for the period of her pregnancy. God doesn't always provide the detailed instructions we might like. Often it's a matter of taking a single step at a time, and trusting the Master to lead on a need-to-know basis.

Was it merely a matter of thanking the angelic visitor for his blessed revelation? Had there been a stirring within, a yearning for more time with this Divine guest? Or could Manoah have been hoping that an extended stay might lead to more of the further advice he desperately sought? We can only guess. Whatever the case, the invitation was offered. "We would like you to stay until we prepare a young goat for you" (13:15). The Angel of the Lord declined the meal, suggesting that it instead be given as a burnt offering to Yahweh. Despite turning down their offer of food, He did stay with the couple a little longer.

The head of the house had one more inquiry to make. "What is your name, so that we may honor you when your word comes true?" (13:17). Manoah still didn't know that he was dealing with God Himself in flesh. To him this was a "man of God," probably a prophet. The messenger demurred. His only response was: "Why do you ask my name? It is beyond understanding" (13:18). Some Bible translators offer an alternative translation from the original Hebrew. They say it may be read as "It is wonderful." Could that be a reference to one of the names given to the Son of God in Isaiah 9:6... "...he will be called Wonderful..."?

Manoah accepted the counsel of the Angel and offered the young goat, and a grain offering, to the Lord. It was at that moment that the guest's prolonged visit came to a rather surreal end. "As the flame blazed up from the altar toward heaven, the Angel of the LORD ascended in the flame" (13:20). The astounded husband and wife fell face down on the ground. When Manoah realized that this heavenly envoy was not to be seen again, he finally understood that they had just had an audience with God Himself!

Thus concludes the extraordinary prologue to the life of Samson. The events which follow, are no less dramatic. Fasten your seatbelts because the ride is not a smooth one! It features more ups and downs than an award winning roller coaster, and will reveal a man of confusing contradictions. Samson is perhaps the utmost example in Scripture of the juxtaposition of spiritual anointing for God's work, and willful pursuit of carnal desires. As confirmed by his inclusion in faith's hall of fame in Hebrews chapter 11, Samson was a man of faith. But according to the record of his life in Judges 13-16, he was also a man driven by fleshly passions. Unfortunately, there are still Samson-like figures among God's people today.

As the boy Samson grew, the Lord blessed him. Judges 13:25 tells us that "...the Spirit of the LORD began to stir him while he was in Mahaneh Dan, between Zorah and Eshtaol." No other details are provided there, but the highly regarded early 18th century Bible Commentator, Matthew Henry, had reason to believe that this location was the site of a military facility of sorts. He asserts that the events of this verse took place "...in the camp of Dan, that is, in the general muster of the trained bands of that tribe, who probably had formed a camp between Zorah and Eshtaol, near the place where Samson lived, to oppose the incursions of the Philistines..."

The Holy Spirit-anointed activities of Samson were in the realm of physical and military conflict, so it would be of no surprise if the powerful stirrings he felt began in this type of setting. What's worth noting even before we recount his supernatural deeds, however, is that he never appeared to serve with any group of soldiers, let alone lead any army. Unlike most of his predecessors during this period of Israel's history, Samson was a loner. I believe that tells us something about his temperament. It was his self-absorption that would bring about his downfall.

It didn't take long for this feature of his personality to march to the forefront of the narrative. Chapter 14 kicks off by saying that "Samson went down to Timnah and saw there a young Philistine woman." *Saw* is a key word not only in the opening verse of this chapter, but throughout the account of his too short life. What we see and how we gaze have a profound impact on our lives, for good or bad. "...the lust of the eyes... comes not from the Father but from the world" (I John 2:16). Samson had a calling born in the heart of God Almighty in Heaven, but a lust conceived in the heart of the god of this world: Satan. Like vinegar and baking soda, the mixture of these two elements would lead to an eruption, though that time was not yet at hand.

So the first recorded event in his life finds Samson traveling several miles from his home in Zorah, into enemy territory at Timnah. What was this rookie judge doing there? We're not told. Perhaps he was on an errand. Maybe he was scouting out the place in preparation for an attack on Israel's oppressors. Or could it be that his wandering eye had led to a restless spirit and a venture into forbidden desires? The aftermath of his trip could lend credence to the latter theory. A young Philistine woman had caught his eye and he returned home with wedding plans on his mind. Samson disrespectfully *demanded* that his mother and father comply with his wishes. "I have seen a Philistine woman in Timnah; now get her for me as my wife" (Judges 14:2).

Samson was not only disrespecting his parents, he was disregarding the Word of God! He was pursuing the very kind of thing that the Lord had warned against in Exodus 34:15,16. "Be careful not to make a treaty with those who live in the land; for when they prostitute themselves to their gods and sacrifice to them, they will invite you and you will eat their sacrifices. And when you choose some of their daughters as wives for your sons and those daughters prostitute themselves to their gods, they will lead your sons to do the same." Likely aware of this divine warning, Samson's parents urged him to instead find a wife among God's people.

Persisting in his wayward intentions, Samson refused to heed their righteous advice. "Get her for me," he insisted, "She's the right one for me" (Judges 14:3). It's not hard to feel the insolence in his words. He was determined to get his own way. Many a godly parent has faced this same frustrating and potentially heartbreaking confrontation with a child who may have come of age, but has not developed true spiritual maturity. Samson was determined to get his own way, and was closed to any wise parental counsel.

It's at this point in the story that a curious parenthetical statement is interjected. Verse 4 informs us that "His parents did not know that this was from the LORD, who was seeking an occasion to confront the Philistines..." Commentators are divided into two schools of thought over this statement. Some believe that it indicates God intended for Samson to marry this Philistine, and actually planted the desire in his heart in order to open a door of opportunity to punish Israel's enemy. Others think the

Lord did not direct or even approve of his action, but nonetheless planned to use it for the benefit of His people.

I'm of the latter opinion. It reminds me of what Joseph once said to his brothers who had years earlier cruelly sold him into slavery... a terrible wrong which ultimately led to a great blessing for both Joseph and his brethren. "You intended to harm me, but God intended it for good..." (Genesis 50:20). God's love for His children sometimes overrides the consequences of our sinful inclinations to accomplish a beneficial divine objective.

This truth evokes a personal childhood memory. My father smoked cigarettes. One day at a family picnic, when I was about 6 or 7, I asked him to let me try one. At first he refused, but I continued to pester him. Eventually he consented, but with a plan in mind. He handed me his lit cigarette and I asked what to do with it. "Put it in your mouth and take a *deep* breath," he instructed. I eagerly followed his instructions, but quickly regretted it. I thought I was dying, and wondered why my uncles and aunts were all laughing about it! I had stupidly wanted to begin a harmful habit, but the effect of my first experiment with tobacco was that I never again touched another cigarette. My desire had been a wrong one, but its momentary fulfillment curbed my temptation for a lifetime.

Manoah and his wife gave in to their son's willful decision, and traveled with him to Timnah to arrange for the marriage. Somewhere along the way Samson and his parents ended up taking different courses for a while. As the young man neared the vineyards of Timnah, he alone came under attack by a fierce predator. This raises two questions. Why did Samson stray from the path his mother and father took, and why did he allow himself to pass so close to a place that could tempt him to break his Nazarite vow? Nazarites were not permitted to consume grapes or anything derived from them, including wine and vinegar.

Reading between the lines may just provide the answers. Knowing that his parents had already attempted to dissuade him from a perilous marriage, Samson probably anticipated their disapproval of a side trip to the vineyard as well. Delinquent living often involves secret journeys. Free-spirit types are inclined toward risky living. You'll likely discover them driving as close to the guard rails as they can, believing they're clever enough to avoid a crash.

Perhaps the lion who roared into Samson's lane was meant as a warning from the Lord. Whatever the case, God protected his servant. His Spirit rushed upon him, and under that anointing Samson killed the lion with no weapon beyond his bare hands. This is the first record of a supernatural endowment of strength for Israel's newest judge. He chose not to tell his parents about it. The entire incident remained concealed from those intermittent travel companions of his.

The wording of Judges 14:7 is quite interesting. It concludes the description of this second journey to Timnah by telling us that Samson "...went down and talked with the woman, and he liked her." Apparently his decision to marry this Philistine girl was based solely on her good looks! Scripture only observes of his first encounter with her that he "saw" her. Evidently, on that factor alone he determined to marry her. Only after he later spoke with her face to face did he even learn that "he liked her." His attraction to his wife-to-be was pretty shallow, and later events would show that his marital commitment was too. This was another indication that the poor judgment Samson exhibited on numerous occasions was usually driven by "the lust of his eyes" (I John 2:16).

Later, on his way to the wedding feast, the groom took a side trip to view the slain lion's carcass. He discovered that bees had nested in it and produced honey. He scooped some out with his hands and ate it along the way, sharing it with his father and mother when he caught up with them. Samson didn't disclose the details about where this tasty treat originated. Those details however, would soon become the mechanism that led to his first real conflict with the Philistines.

Arriving at the wedding feast, Samson was given 30 male companions from among the local Philistine clan. As we previously mentioned, the tale of Israel's strongman paints a picture of someone inclined to be a loner. So it should not surprise us that he probably attended the celebration without the company of friends from back home in Zorah. That may be why his wife's extended family, or her village, saw a need to supply some buddies for Samson.

It's not clear what activities were expected of these men other than simply providing companionship for Samson, but he decided to have some fun with them... or was it his aim to have some selfish fun at their expense? Recalling his discovery of honey in the lion's remains, he created a riddle to be the basis of a wager. If they could solve the riddle by the close of the week-long wedding feast, Samson would give them 30 sets of clothes. If not, they would pay him 30 sets of clothes. They took him up on his offer, and so the riddle was recited. "Out of the eater, something to eat; out of the strong, something sweet" (14:14).

Obviously the riddle baffled his groomsmen, because by the fourth day they were still coming up empty. The group was in no mood to lose a bet to this lowly Jew. That would be an insult to their position as Israel's overlords! They accused the bride of using the feast as an occasion to rob them. Their anger was so intense that they threatened to burn Samson's wife and family to death if she didn't wheedle the answer out of her husband. Some *friendly* companions this bunch turned out to be!

Faced with a death threat, Samson's wife set out to save the day by using her most effective feminine powers of persuasion against him. Weeping violently she cried: "You hate me! You don't really love me." She went on to lament: "You've given my people a riddle, but you haven't told me the answer" (14:16). Her husband protested that he hadn't even told his own parents the answer, so why should he explain it to her? But she would not be denied. The spigot of her tears had been opened wide, and would remain so for what was left of their wedding feast. She tightened the emotional clamps until Samson surrendered.

On the final day of the festivities Samson told her what she wanted to hear, and she promptly passed it on to the men of the wedding party. As the deadline for the conclusion of the wager approached, they strutted before this Israelite nobody to arrogantly declare the answer they had stolen through coercion. Samson was livid! He made it clear that he knew they had won the bet by cheating. "If you had not plowed with my heifer, you would not have solved my riddle" (14:18). They would get their 30 suits, but these malicious Philistines would pay the price for it.

As He had when the lion attacked, the Holy Spirit descended on God's chosen servant once more. Supernaturally empowered, Samson journeyed about 20 miles to one of the enemy's major cities (Ashkelon), slew 30 men, stripped them, and gave their clothes to his 30 treacherous wedding companions. Unaware of the death threat they'd hurled at his new wife, he was angry at her as well for her seemingly inexcusable betrayal. Having paid off his gambling debts, Samson deserted his bride and stormed off to his parents house. And you thought it was only *wives* who went home to their mothers.

Among other things, Samson's reaction to his wife's behavior demonstrated how little he understood about personal relationships in general, and the marriage covenant in particular. The motivations for the actions of family and friends aren't always what we might think they are. Samson should have reined in his anger and tried to talk things out with his bride, rather than run away. The same can often be said for many married couples. Love is not just a feeling, it's a commitment.

We're not told how long the young husband stayed away from his wife, but it was certainly long enough for her father to believe he wasn't coming back. Accordingly, he gave his daughter as wife to one of Samson's wedding attendants. When the wandering husband finally returned to see his bride, this news came as a shock. The father offered her younger sister (whom he declared was even better looking) to a very disturbed now ex-husband. Samson would have none of it. His temper had risen to the boiling point and he determined to take revenge. "This time I have a right to get even with the Philistines; I will really harm them" (15:3).

Since it was harvest time, he devised an attack that would hit them where it really hurt. Samson gathered 300 foxes (or jackals) and used them to spread a blaze that devoured their wheat fields, vineyards, and olive groves. When the Philistines learned that it was the Timnites son-in-law who had devastated their crops because his wife had been given to another, they did exactly what they had threatened earlier... they burned father and daughter to death. That only led to more anger and more revenge from Samson. He attacked and killed many Philistines, then retreated to a cave near Lehi in the territory of Israel's tribe of Judah.

A Philistine army soon camped nearby, and when the men of Judah asked why they had come, their answer was "We have come to take Samson prisoner... to do to him as he did to us" (15:10). We might expect these fellow Israelites to take Samson's side against a common enemy. Instead, they spoke to him in fear. "Don't you realize that that the Philistines are rulers over us? What have you done to us?" (15:11). Then again, maybe there was more than fear at work. Samson was a loner and acted largely in his own personal interests. It could also be that the tribe of Judah had no interest in joining forces with this seemingly rogue Danite. Whatever their full reasons were, they had come to tie Samson up and turn him over to the Philistines in order to save their own necks.

The suspect made no attempt to resist arrest by his Jewish brethren, making but one request. "Swear to me that you won't kill me yourselves" (15:12). The men of Judah agreed. They bound his arms and hands with two newly made ropes and escorted him out of the cave toward the Philistines. His unwittingly jubilant enemies had no idea what was about to hit them.

As Samson drew near the Philistine camp at Lehi, their troops rushed toward him shouting their war cries. Thousands of hardened soldiers were about to overwhelm a single Israelite. No one in their right mind would expect anything other than the immediate capture and/or execution of this lone warrior. But then, Samson was not in his *right* mind at that moment. The Spirit of Yahweh took control of his mind and body. He effortlessly snapped the cords that bound him, and reached for a fresh donkey jawbone he found nearby. Wielding this makeshift weapon against the refined military hardware of the Philistine army, he struck down a thousand of their soldiers!

In the aftermath of this astounding triumph, Samson once more demonstrated evidence that his God-given gifts may have reached beyond his supernatural physical strength. His post-victory speech hinted at his being something of a word meister. He had earlier created a catchy riddle for his wedding companions, then an intriguing retort when they offered the solution coerced from his wife. This time he seemed to be using a play on words to announce his conquest. "With a donkey's jawbone I have made donkeys of them. With a donkey's jawbone I have killed a thousand men" (15:16). The phrase "I have made donkeys of them" might also be translated "I have made a heap or two of them," since the Hebrew word for *donkey* sounds like the Hebrew word for *heap*.

The extended battle left him tired and severely dehydrated with nothing to drink, so Samson prayed. It was the first of only three recorded prayers uttered by him. "You have given your servant this great victory. Must I now die of thirst and fall into the hands of the uncircumcised?" (15:18). This plea illustrates the disparity between Samson's higher calling and lower nature. He gratefully acknowledged that the victory he celebrated was from the Lord. Yet his request for water to quench his thirst was constructed as a sour complaint. In answer to his prayer God created a spring where there had been none before, and His weary servant drank and was revitalized. Both the site of the defeat of the Philistines and the location of the new spring of water were given names to memorialize the intervention of the Almighty.

Judges chapter 16 begins with a brief account of another example of Samson's lustful eyes... and his divinely endowed strength. He traveled to another of the Philistine's chief cities, Gaza, "where he saw a prostitute" (16:1). This time marriage was not even a faint notion. Samson was merely out to indulge his sexual urges. He spent the night with this woman satisfying his illicit desires in disobedience to God's laws. No possibly legitimate objective for his visit to Gaza is even hinted at in the text.

The citizens of this enemy enclave got wind that their antagonist was in town and determined to take advantage of this chance to kill him. They decided to wait until morning to make their move, but Samson arose in the middle of the night to leave. Did he suspect the plot against him and hope to escape under the cover of darkness? Had God revealed their strategy to him? Is it possible he came under conviction, and fled the scene of his sin prompted by the remorse of a smitten conscience? We can only hope it was the latter.

Samson headed straight to the gate of the city where his foes were waiting for him. We're not told why the

Philistine guards didn't stop him. Maybe they'd fallen asleep or somehow the Lord had blinded their eyes. Perhaps Samson quickly overpowered them. We do know that he took hold of the gate; doors, posts, and bar; and carted it off to the top of the hill facing the Jewish city of Hebron. Such gates were built for military security and may have been as large as twelve feet high. Tearing one from the ground and carrying it a great distance would be more than an impressive feat, it would likely be humanly impossible. But Samson's deed was not powered by manly muscles. His strength was fueled by Holy Spirit adrenaline!

This incident at Gaza displayed the accelerating rate of Samson's downhill spiritual trek. His self-absorbed lifestyle was taking greater and greater precedence over the Lord's agenda. It was about to lead to his final ill-chosen romantic escapade, and the resulting defeat at the hands of those from whom God had called him to deliver Israel. Enter the person whose name is invariably associated with that of Samson: Delilah.

The Nazarite leader discovered his third and last romance in the Valley of Sorek. This area was known for it's "choice vineyards." In fact, that's the meaning of the name Sorek. Once more we see Samson pushing the envelope at the very least... maybe even partaking of the fruit forbidden by his holy consecration to the Lord. Those who play near fire will eventually be burned, and he would soon experience more than one meaning of the term "third degree." For Samson, *falling* in love with the wrong woman would lead to a much more destructive *tumble*.

The account doesn't plainly disclose Delilah's background. She may even have been Jewish, though that seems unlikely given her pivotal role in the Philistine conspiracy against Samson. Immediately following the first mention of her name, the Philistine rulers arrive on the scene to enlist her as a very personal spy on their behalf. Each of them offered her 1,100 shekels of silver if she could uncover the secret of Samson's power. At the price of silver as this book is penned, that would be nearly $10,000 per ruler! The fact that they sought "the *secret* of his great strength" lends credence to the idea that Samson did not appear to be unusually muscle-bound. Otherwise the source of his strength would not be secret, but rather obvious. Delilah agreed to their proposal and the ruse was on.

Delilah's approach was so blatant that only a fool could not see through it. Unfortunately, Samson had become that fool. His eyes had been so absorbed by lust that he was blind to the obvious reality of what was happening. His wisdom had been so waylaid by his diminishing fear of the Lord that he had descended into the dark caverns of stupidity. Under the thin guise of love, Delilah requested: "Tell me the secret of your great strength and how you can be tied up and subdued" (16:6). If the first part of the appeal didn't stir suspicions, the second part certainly should have raised Samson's eyebrows. Why would his lover want to know how he could be captured? His blindness to the intent of her inquiry demonstrates the depths to which self-deceit can bury a man.

Samson's initial response might have reflected some residual sense of caution. He suggested that if he were tied up with seven fresh thongs (or bow strings) his strength would abate. Delilah quickly tested the veracity of his statement by tying him up herself with fresh thongs provided by the Philistine rulers. Then with enemy combatants hidden and at the ready in her home, she cried: "Samson, the Philistines are upon you!" (16:9). God's errant servant snapped the cords easily and instantly. His girlfriend subsequently protested that he'd made a fool of her, and repeated her plea for the knowledge that would make her rich.

Surely Samson's eyes would now be opened to her duplicity... how could he miss what was so transparent? Yet he remained a dupe of his enemies. Again she pressed the question, complaining of his lies to her. Apparently some level of prudence still drifted on the surface of his weakened reservoir of resolve. This time Samson claimed that new ropes would render him powerless. Delilah repeated her previous actions with the revised means of restraint, but the end result was the same. Samson snapped the ropes as though they were skinny threads.

Delilah hoped the third time would be the charm. Once more she protested that her boyfriend continued to make a fool of her. In reality it was Samson who continued to make a fool of himself. His resolve weakening by the moment, he began to come perilously close to revealing the actual source of his might. Into the picture entered the most noticeable sign of his Nazarite vow: his uncut hair. It was an odd explanation he offered to Delilah. "If you weave the seven braids of my head into the fabric on the loom and tighten it with the pin, I'll become as weak as any other man" (16:13). Waiting until the strongman fell asleep this time, she followed his instructions. Still, as before, when the Philistines came out of hiding Samson easily broke free.

As with the wife of his short-lived marriage, Delilah turned to one of her most effectual female wiles. She accused him of *not loving her.* His unwillingness to confide in her was incontrovertible evidence of this, she reasoned. At least with his late wife, her efforts stemmed from death threats. Delilah was in it for the money. From that point on this traitorous mistress turned to nagging him day after day after day. Scripture describes Samson's reaction to this relentless assault with these words: "... he was tired to death" (16:16). The inspired writer could hardly have chosen a more apt expression. Unaltered by spiritual renewal, the product of his weariness would be both literally and figuratively the grave. As he wore down, Samson surrendered both the mystery of his strength and his holy vow to this downward slide. In essence he declared to his disloyal sweetheart, "Shave my head (ending my Nazarite vow) and my power will be gone."

Delilah alerted the Philistine rulers one final time, and they arrived with the bounty they had promised her. This time the Bible says that she "put him to sleep on her lap" (16:19). How imprudent had this once divinely ordained judge become! One way or another he allowed himself to be lulled into slumber by his betrayer. Samson was so unconscious that a stranger was able to clip his braids without awakening him. Was he that heavy a sleeper? Had Delilah drugged him? Or was this deep slumber simply an extension of his spiritual stupor?

A fourth time Delilah exclaimed to Samson that the Philistines were upon him. Rousing himself from intense sleep, he expected to shake himself as he had so many times before, anticipating that the power of God would free him from his bondage and grant him triumph over his foes.

It was not to be. Some of the saddest words in all of the Bible reveal the expansive reach of the deceptive spiritual weed which had sunk it's roots into the garden of his heart and overtaken it. Judges 16:20 records of Samson that "... *he did not know* that the LORD had left him." I'm reminded of David's lament when he received word of the death of King Saul and Prince Jonathan. "How the mighty have fallen in battle!" (I Samuel 1:25).

We can go through the motions which have become part and parcel of our spiritual history, but if the Holy Spirit has departed they become nothing but empty rituals. The power of God will have departed our lives. The most pathetic aspect of Samson's condition was that he didn't even realize that his longtime Divine Companion was no longer with him. His self-centered lifestyle had so captivated his mind that he was no longer sensitive to the voice and Presence of Yahweh. The effects of sin usually consume our souls so gradually that we're not aware of what we've lost until our sudden capture at the hands of the enemy awakens us to the truth that our once precious treasure has been progressively pilfered by our own self-will!

Was it simply the *Manifest Presence* of God that Samson's sin had relinquished, or had his sinful ways actually broken covenant with Yahweh to the point where he'd lost the Lord's *Covenant Presence*? I confess I have no certain answer to that question. In my mind it might be either. I am, however, confident that in any case the path for restoration of God's Presence was ultimately open to this wayward leader.

Meanwhile the Philistines, wasted no time in attempting to assure themselves that they would never again be victims of Samson's once mighty muscles. Having already shorn his locks, they next gouged out his eyes. Even if he somehow regained his strength, it would be of limited use without his sight. How sad, and yet how significant was his condition. God's servant had allowed his eyes to lead him astray, and now a large part of the price he paid for his backsliding was the loss of his vision. Indulging the lust of the eyes is no harmless pastime, my friend.

They hurried the humiliated man off to Gaza, strapped bronze shackles to his limbs, then put him to work at the prison grindstone. Day after drudging day passed as Samson suffered alone in this dreary workhouse. Yet something hopeful was happening. Judges 16:22 is a sentence that is both gloriously simple and simply glorious: "But the hair on his head began to grow again after it had been shaved." Hallelujah! Something was stirring in Samson and it wasn't just his hair follicles. The refurbishing of his scalp was just symbolic of another revitalization. I believe that spiritual processes were at work, hidden within his soul. Israel's fallen leader was reassessing his life and priorities. Repentance for sin was taking place. Yearning for the lost Presence of the Lord was moving his heart. A righteous anger against the enemy of God's children was pulsing through his arteries. A holy faith rose up in him!

The idolatrous Philistines were convinced that their victory over Samson reflected the superiority of their god Dagon over Israel's God, Yahweh. The rulers declared a celebration to honor Dagon, and Samson was the guest of *dis*honor. A large crowd gathered to offer sacrifice and praise to their false deity. At the height of their revelry they called for Samson to be brought out for entertainment purposes. Scripture tells us he "performed for them," but rest assured he wasn't singing and dancing, nor was he executing feats of strength. Chances are the amusement of the crowd involved humiliating their captive, perhaps by cruelties like sucker-punching him or placing obstacles in his way to trip him up in his blindness.

While they roared with laughter at his expense, the victim of their ridicule was silently developing a plan that would bring the glory back to the true God of all mankind. The temple of Dagon, which was the scene of the Philistine's festivities, was supported by huge pillars. Perhaps Samson was familiar with its structure from his previous visit to Gaza. Maybe he'd even purposefully scouted it out. What is apparent is that he understood that to collapse the pillars was to bring down the entire edifice. He made a request of the Philistine servant who led him around. "Put me where I can feel the pillars that support the temple, so that I may lean against them" (16:26). Samson then prayed, "O Sovereign LORD, remember me. O God, please strengthen me just once more, and let me with one blow get revenge on the Philistines for my two eyes" (16:28).

Positioning himself between the primary pillars, Samson placed his right hand on one, and his left hand on the other. Then he breathed his final prayer: "Let me die with the Philistines!" (16:30). The request of the repentant judge of Israel was granted by his Heavenly Master, and the temple of Dagon became a pile of rubble. Yahweh's Presence had descended in power upon Samson. We're not told how many of the cruel oppressors of God's people died in this destruction, but two facts are cited. There were approximately 3,000 people on just the roof alone at the time (16:27), and Samson "killed many more when he died than while he lived" (16:30).

It was likely with a mixture of sorrow and pride that Samson's extended family claimed his body from the ruins in Gaza. His carnal indulgences had ultimately cost him his life, but he'd made things right with the Lord and closed the book on his earthly history with the greatest victory of his career. They buried him back home in his father's tomb. He'd led Israel for 20 years. So looking back, what lessons should we learn from Samson's life?

Lesson 1: The callings of God are His sovereign choices. Samson was chosen to be Israel's judge before he was born. Jeremiah was called to be a prophet before his birth (Jeremiah 1:5). Jacob was chosen over Esau to be the father of the Lord's special people before either was born (Romans 9:10-12). Godly character is essential to continuing to walk in divine blessing, but divine callings are established in heaven, not in human minds. We may wonder at times why God has called certain people (including ourselves) to certain positions, but our opinion doesn't matter... only God's sovereign decisions matter. Gifts and callings are from the Lord. What we do with them is largely in our hands. Perfection is not a prerequisite for a calling to leadership or ministry, though the development of integrity is vital to its proper function.

Lesson 2: The Lord's anointing overcomes human weakness. Scripture makes it clear that Samson's amazing strength was not native to his earthly body. It was a supernatural endowment resulting from the Holy Spirit descending on him. Though each of us is born with natural gifts, the Manifest Presence of God provides power that surpasses the limitations of these innate abilities. When divine anointing empowers us, He does the work, and He should get the glory. Let's not forget that with all his shortcomings, Samson was a man of faith. That faith enabled him to do mighty deeds.

In his second letter to the Corinthian believers, the Apostle Paul taught them that "...we have this treasure in jars of clay to show that this all-surpassing power is from God and not from us" (II Corinthians 4:7). Later in that same epistle he related how he had asked the Lord to deliver him from what he called "a thorn in the flesh." God told His servant that His grace was strong was enough to enable him to deal with it: "...for my power is made perfect in weakness." Paul responded, "Therefore I will boast all the more gladly about my weaknesses, so that Christ's power may rest on me" (II Corinthians 12:9).

Lesson 3: We need to carefully guard our eyes. The same goes for our remaining senses, of course. Their intake can also lead to ungodly sensual desires. There's no question, however, that sight extends the most commanding influence over our thoughts and behavior. Samson was repeatedly led astray by what he saw. In his case it was predominately sexual lust that was aroused. He would have done well to practice a precept from Job's personal manual of righteous living: "I made a covenant with my eyes not to look lustfully at a girl" (Job 31:1).

In today's media saturated society it's even easier than in Samson's era to engage in fornicatious and adulterous fantasies. While we can't walk around with our eyes shut, we can minimize our risks by controlling where our eyes might wander and on what they might fix themselves. Images that excite wrong desires should be avoided whenever possible. Even when we can't help but see something sinfully alluring, we need to avoid that lingering or second look. Everyday encounters can also feed the monster inside us: the old fleshly nature. It only takes a moment for legitimate appreciation of beauty to morph into illegitimate sexual desire.

At that point the lingering or second look can take place in the mind's eye, rather than the physical eye. A mental image can be just as powerful as an actual one. Many years ago a friend confided in me that once in a moment of weakness he'd made the mistake of viewing an X-rated film. His expression of regret revealed the intensity of visual memory. He informed me that: "It only takes an *hour* to watch a pornographic movie, but a *lifetime* to forget it." So to borrow a piece of advice from the old *Mayberry RFD* television series character, Barney Fife: it's best to "Nip it in the bud!"

Lust of the eyes however, is not confined to sexual appetites. Anything that appeals to our vision can produce illicit lust. Not that all desires which stem from what we see are evil. God has created many good things for us to enjoy: natural beauty, good food, pleasant homes, etc. It's when what we see produces yearning that is out of Biblical balance, or is for things that are inherently evil, or are not rightfully ours, that it leads to sin. When our longings become covetous and greedy it spells trouble. James 1:14,15 warns us: "…but each one is tempted when, by his own evil desire, he is dragged away and enticed. Then, after desire has conceived, it gives birth to sin; and sin, when it is full-grown, gives birth to death."

Lesson 4: We need each other. Fellowship among believers is a necessary element of our walk with the Lord. For the most part, Samson was a Lone Ranger…

without even a Tonto by his side! He was disrespectful to his parents, insensitive and unforgiving of his young wife, and virtually without friends. As a result, he missed out on the help that can come from those relationships. After creating the first human, God recognized "It is not good for the man to be alone" (Genesis 2:18). The Psalmist later reminded us that "God sets the lonely in families" (Psalm 68:6). From righteous relationships we gain prayers, encouragement, correction, feedback, accountability, and more. Close spiritual family and friends just might have changed Samson's fate. With such help he may have avoided the tragic loss of the Lord's Presence.

Lesson 5: Disobedience will ultimately rob us of our greatest treasure. It erodes our sensitivity to the voice and Presence of God. Isaiah 59:2 explains what happens. "But your iniquities have separated you from your God; your sins have hidden his face from you, so that he will not hear." Obedience leads to blessing; disobedience to curses (Deuteronomy 11:26-28). Persistence in sin puts distance between God and His people. The process can be so gradual that we don't even realize what's happening. Samson's disobedience eventually made him so spiritually numb that he wasn't even aware that the Lord had left him. Sin is a dangerous game we can not afford to play!

Lesson 6: Repentance is the key that opens the door for mercy and restoration. Understand, my friend, repentance is not simply saying you're sorry and asking for forgiveness. It goes deeper than being unhappy that you've suffered the consequences of your sin. Repentance is a godly regret that you've done wrong and have offended God. It reaches beyond seeking forgiveness, to asking the Lord to help you change your behavior... to make a 180 degree turn around from your old sinful conduct. That's the place to which I believe Samson came after he finally realized he'd traded his holy heritage for carnal debauchery.

The wonderful truth is that the Lord is a merciful God. His desire is to send no one to eternal judgment. "He is patient with you, not wanting anyone to perish, but everyone to come to repentance" (II Peter 3:9). James 2:13 says it even more succinctly: "Mercy triumphs over judgment!" Yahweh was not licking his chops, excited at the prospect of tossing Samson into hell. God was waiting for his servant's turn around with arms opened wide. When that moment arrived, the Holy Spirit not only re-entered Samson's life, the Lord endowed him one last time with supernatural strength to hand the enemy the worst defeat in Samson's lifetime!

We're just as capable as Samson of squandering the treasure of God's Presence. But thank the Lord He's just as willing to forgive and restore us as He was to do so for Israel's backslidden judge. If God has been driven from your life by your constant disobedience, the solution is straightforward. If you want Him back, tell Him so. Repent of your sins and experience the return of His precious Presence!

CHAPTER 3

DON'T LET IT GO TO YOUR HEAD

Following the death of the renowned King Solomon, his son and heir, Rehoboam, accepted some poor advice from his peers and became a harsh monarch. He rejected the wisdom of the elders and refused to listen to the appeals of his people to deal more kindly and fairly with them. The result was that most of his subjects rejected him, and the Jewish nation split into two separate countries. From that point forward the tribe of Judah and part of the tribe of Benjamin became the Southern Kingdom known as Judah. They continued under the jurisdiction of Rehoboam and the ensuing heirs in the line of King David. The remaining tribes formed the Northern Kingdom called Israel. Starting with their first king, Jeroboam, (who had earlier rebelled against Solomon) they would serve a number of sovereigns from various families over the centuries.

Both dominions would experience good and bad leadership, although Judah had more of the former and Israel more of the latter. One of the most revered monarchs of this era was King Hezekiah of Judah. Hezekiah's godly reign was sandwiched between that of two ungodly kings: his father, Ahaz, and his son, Manassah. You'll find significant portions of Hezekiah's life detailed in three Old Testament books. In all, there are eleven chapters devoted to his story in II Kings, II Chronicles, and Isaiah. A couple of brief but useful additional mentions of Hezekiah are made in Proverbs and Jeremiah. An interesting twist to his tale later in life is why he needs to be included in this study.

In the various Bible accounts of Hezekiah's life we'll learn much about the kind of person he was. By far the most telling statements concerning his character are found in II Kings 18:5,6. "Hezekiah trusted in the LORD, the God of Israel. There was no one like him among all the kings of Judah, either before him or after him. He held fast to the LORD and did not cease to follow him; he kept the commands the LORD had given Moses." Of course, the declaration that "there was no one like him among all the kings of Judah" leaves out the likes of David and Solomon since they reigned over the whole nation, not just the later limited Southern Kingdom of Judah. Still, that assessment puts Hezekiah's stock above such righteous rulers of Judah as Asa, Jehoshaphat, and Josiah.

The aforementioned brief references to Hezekiah in Proverbs and Jeremiah reinforce the image of his righteous character. Proverbs 25:1 introduces a listing of Holy Spirit inspired maxims with this statement: "These are more proverbs of Solomon, copied by the men of Hezekiah king of Judah..." This short passage demonstrates the value Hezekiah placed on the preservation and propagation of

Holy Scripture, instructing his servants to make sure these truths of God were not lost to ensuing generations.

Jeremiah 26:17-19 chronicles an event which took place long after Hezekiah's passing, and tells us something more of the king's reverence for God's Word. When the prophet Jeremiah was threatened with execution for divine prophesies of harsh judgment against Judah, wise leaders defended him by citing Hezekiah's attitude toward an earlier prophet of God. "Some of the elders of the land stepped forward and said to the entire assembly of people, Micah of Moresheth prophesied in the days of Hezekiah king of Judah. He told all the people of Judah, 'This is what the Lord Almighty says: Zion will be plowed like a field, Jerusalem will become a heap of rubble, the temple hill a mound overgrown with thickets. Did Hezekiah king of Judah or anyone else in Judah put him to death? Did not Hezekiah fear the Lord and seek his favor? And did not the Lord relent, so that he did not bring the disaster he pronounced against them?'" Hezekiah accepted the Word of the Lord even when it was unpleasant, and knew how to rightly respond to it.

It's apparent from our introductory preview of Hezekiah that he was an upright man, honored by God and subsequently revered by his subjects. The earlier quoted summation of his life taken from II Kings chapter 18, presents him as a model believer and leader. As the full narrative of his reign unfolds, we'll find out that he was nevertheless a flawed human being like the rest of us. So as we study his story we'll see desirable traits we ought to emulate, and discover shortcomings we should seek to avoid. We'll also gain more understanding about those times in our own experience when it seems the Lord's Presence is nowhere to be found.

Two major storylines dominate the account of Hezekiah's kingship while a few related subplots provide indispensable insights as well. Although the time in Hezekiah's reign at which the primary events occurred is noted, the other happenings are neither clearly dated nor necessarily recounted in chronological order. At times that leaves us in the realm of speculation as to some details, but it doesn't confuse the main messages of his life. There's a lot to learn, so let's get started.

We'll begin the telling of his tale with a glimpse into the ungodly atmosphere in which Hezekiah grew up. His homeland of the Southern Kingdom of Judah had been declining spiritually for more than two centuries, although at a slower pace than that of the Northern Kingdom of Israel. His father, King Ahaz, was a considerable contributor to that appalling deterioration. Hezekiah was eight or nine years old when his father ascended to the throne. Early recollections of the relatively righteous rule of his grandfather Jotham would have been minimal compared to the images burned into his memory by the sixteen years of his father's regrettable reign.

To say that Ahaz's leadership was a poor model for the young prince who would one day succeed him is an understatement. Ahaz *turned away* from the worship of Yahweh, the God of Israel. In defiance of the Law of the Lord, he *turned to* the false gods of the pagans around him. Most repulsive was his embrace of the Phoenician demonic deity, Molech. This led to Ahaz sacrificing his own infant sons by slowly burning them to death in the arms of the superheated metallic image of Molech. One can hardly imagine the impact that such a cruel fate, suffered by *his own brothers*, would have had on young Hezekiah.

In time of war Ahaz allied Judah with the heathen Assyrian Empire, stripping riches from the Temple of the Lord in Jerusalem to help pay for this military protection. Under the influence of the Assyrian king, he had a pagan altar copied and placed in the Temple. Eventually he closed the House of God altogether, setting up idolatrous sacrificial altars on most every street corner in the Holy City. His disastrous pact with Assyria ultimately came back to bite him, but he never seemed to learn his lesson. Not one single positive comment on the reign of Ahaz is found anywhere in the Bible!

When Ahaz died, his 25 year old heir succeeded him on the throne of Judah. According to the historical record in II Chronicles chapters 29 through 31, Hezekiah wasted no time in correcting the course of the kingdom. This sudden and radical change in spiritual direction might have left some observers with a severe case of whiplash! It was a 180 degree swing away from idolatry and back to the only true God.

One wonders how such righteous character had developed in young Hezekiah while growing up under a wicked regime. The stark contrast between the leadership styles of Ahaz and his son Hezekiah reminds us once more that we need not be simply the product of our environment. Though the culture that surrounds us has the power to influence our personalities, individual decisions ultimately determine who we become. Standing against the tide of ungodliness which had been engulfing his world, Hezekiah made right choices.

Three full chapters in II Chronicles describe the first of the two biggest events of Hezekiah's nearly three decades of rule. Such relatively extensive coverage of the flurry surrounding the restoration of the divinely ordained worship of Yahweh confirms the monumental significance of this turnaround. It transformed depraved spiritual apostasy into godly spiritual ecstasy. Though personally far removed from such Old Testament traditions, I find myself deeply moved when I read the account of that generation's revival. A spirit of shared joy stirs, and a longing for a New Testament renewal of the Lord's Majestic Presence in my own generation rises in me.

That the freshman king gave top priority to this task is evidenced at the outset by the timeline cited in II Chronicles 29:3. "In the first month of the first year of his reign, he opened the doors of the temple of the LORD and repaired them." Hezekiah astutely understood that unless the God of Abraham, Isaac, and Jacob was restored to His rightful throne, Hezekiah's own throne would be of little benefit to his people. God give us leaders like that in every institution of society! What a difference it would make!

The king quickly called a meeting of the priests and Levites to get them started on this noble project. We would normally expect a nation's spiritual leaders to urge the civil ones to honor God with their activities. On this occasion it was the reverse. Imagine what would happen in our own homeland if the leaders of our government urged church leaders to help restore the rightful place of the Lord in society. Could it be that we've too often voted the wrong kind of people into political power? Have we chosen leaders after our own wayward hearts?

Speaking from in front of the Temple gates, Hezekiah commanded the Levites to consecrate themselves and the place of worship to Yahweh. He recounted how their fathers had turned away from the Lord, defiled the Temple, and ultimately shut it down. He rightly blamed the deaths of their soldiers and the captivity of wives and daughters at the hands of their enemies, on the nation's backslidden condition. Their rebellion against God had roused His fearful anger and judgment. They were paying the price for their unfaithfulness.

Hezekiah went beyond requiring the consecration of the Levites and the Temple. "Now I intend to make a covenant with the LORD, the God of Israel, so that his fierce anger will turn away from us" (II Chronicles 29:10). He had seen the devastating effects of Israel's abandonment of the terms of God's covenant with them. He had just rehearsed them for the priests and Levites. Hezekiah wanted no part in a half-hearted commitment to the Lord. He was pursuing a covenant: a binding pledge to walk in obedience to the Word of God.

Hezekiah remembered what Yahweh had spoken to His people centuries earlier through Moses. After predicting the terrible consequences should future generations of Israelites corrupt their faith and turn to idols, God had held out the promise of blessed restoration. "But if from there you seek the LORD your God, you will find him if you look for him with all your heart and with all your soul. When you are in distress and all these things have happened to you, then in later days you will return to the LORD your God and obey him. For the LORD your God is a merciful God; he will not abandon or destroy you or forget the covenant with your forefathers, which he confirmed to them by oath" (Deuteronomy 4:29-31).

This devoted king was determined to renew their end of the bargain. Unfaithfulness had cost them not only defeat and captivity, they had lost the precious *Covenant Presence* of the Lord. The Presence of God was the chief blessing of the Covenant... the one from which all other blessings flowed. Through the mercy of the Lord and the return to faith and obedience of the chosen race, Hezekiah intended to make backsliding a thing of the past. His heart's cry was much like that of his ancestor David. "Do not cast me from your presence or take your Holy Spirit from me" (Psalm 51:11).

Hezekiah challenged the priests and Levites to renew their ministry before the Lord, reminding them that God Himself had honored their tribe by calling them to this special service. The king's words resonated deep in their spirits, and they immediately "set to work" (II Chronicles 29:12). They gathered more of their ministering brethren and consecrated themselves according to the Law of God.

Ahaz had defiled the Temple, and now his son had ordered them to purify it. Everything unclean... anything the Word of God had forbidden... anything devoted to the worship of false gods... was removed from the House of the Lord. It was cast into the Kidron Valley, an area which had become, among other things, a dumping ground for defilement. Modern archeologists who later excavated it discovered untold centuries worth of rubbish covering the ground to a depth of many feet. That's where the remnants of the idolatry of our rebellious past belong: in the town dump!

In 16 days the Levites completed the project, following up the purging of unclean things, by purifying for holy use the long neglected sacred utensils that belonged in the Temple. They reported their accomplishments to Hezekiah, who then gathered the civil leaders together and headed for the House of God to do their part in pursuing revival. The first order of business was to seek full Biblical repentance. Godly sorrow for sin was a proper start, but it provided no cleansing. "…Without the shedding of blood there is no forgiveness" (Hebrews 9:22). Though the blood of the Son of God Himself would in due course be the final provision, under the Old Covenant that forgiveness came temporarily through the blood of a sacrificial animal which would be the "sin offering."

In this matter the *leaders* of the people did just what their title implied… they *led*. True leaders recognize that responsibility. In his Thanksgiving Proclamation to the American people in 1863, President Abraham Lincoln became more that just a *political* leader, he acted as a *spiritual* leader. Acknowledging that the Civil War which desolated the country was likely a judgment from God for it's presumptuous sins, he began his public statement with these words:

> "It is the duty of nations as well as of men to owe their dependence upon the overruling power of God; to confess their sins and transgressions in humble sorrow, yet with assured hope that genuine repentance will lead to mercy and pardon; and to recognize the sublime truth, announced in the Holy Scriptures and proven by all history, that

those nations are blessed whose God is
the Lord."

We can easily anticipate the censorious reaction of the media and others if a modern president dared to speak to the nation from such a plainly Biblical perspective today! Yet any society that wants to enjoy real happiness and prosperity must turn away from sin and back to the ways of the Lord. That's what Hezekiah and those in other positions of governmental power did as a requisite example for the rest of Jerusalem and Judah. The Jewish leaders acted in obedience to the instructions for the sin offering found in Leviticus 4:15: "The elders of the community are to lay their hands on the bull's head before the LORD, and the bull shall be slaughtered before the LORD." This act was symbolic of the transfer of the sins of the people to the sacrificial animal, whose life's blood paid the price for their sins. Thus the nation moved from repentance to restoration.

The sin offering paved the way for the burnt offerings, which represented dedication to the service of God, and the joyful music of praise featuring the singers and instrumentalists. Then the king and company fell to their knees in worship. Having fulfilled the requirements of the Law, Hezekiah essentially declared the House of the Lord open for business. An abundant flow of more burnt offerings, fellowship offerings, and drink offerings began as "...the service of the temple of the LORD was reestablished" (II Chronicles 29:35). The episode closed on a glorious note: "Hezekiah and all the people rejoiced at what God had brought about for his people, because it was done so quickly" (II Chronicles 29:36).

We all know that Martin Luther King, Jr. had a dream. He wanted to see a nation divided between black and white come together. In a sense Hezekiah had a similar dream. Not content with the restoration of the Temple in Jerusalem, the king wanted to see the divided Northern and Southern kingdoms of Israel joined as one. Political unification was not his primary concern. Spiritual unification was. Hezekiah dreamt of all the children of Abraham becoming one through their worship of the Living God who had given them birth.

The vehicle for this harmony in worship would be the Passover celebration. Also known as the Feast of Unleavened Bread, it was the first of all the sacred festivals observed by the Jews, having been established by the Lord even before the Law was given to Moses. It commemorated the deliverance of the children of Israel from their bondage in Egypt. The Passover Lamb, which was central to the feast, anticipated the cross of Calvary, and Jesus Christ as "…the Lamb of God who takes away the sin of the world" (John 1:29). According to the Lord's command, the sacrifice of the Passover Lamb and the ensuing celebration was to take place nowhere "…except in the place he (Yahweh) will choose as a dwelling for his Name" (Deuteronomy 16:6). That exclusive place was Mount Zion: Jerusalem!

After the nation of Israel divided into two separate kingdoms early in the reign of Rehoboam, the ten tribes of the northern kingdom crowned a man named Jeroboam as their king. He quickly turned them away from Yahweh, creating two golden calves as their gods, telling the people they need not go to Jerusalem to the Temple to worship. Eventually the city of Samaria was established as the capitol of Israel, and a motley succession of kings ruled from there for approximately two centuries. Now Hezekiah's heart reached out to his backslidden brethren.

A letter of invitation to the Passover was delivered by the king's couriers not only to the towns in the southern kingdom of Judah, but throughout the northern kingdom of Israel as well. Though widely met with scorn and ridicule outside Hezekiah's domain, a number of people in Israel responded to the tug of the Holy Spirit on their hearts. "Nevertheless, some men of Asher, Manasseh and Zebulun humbled themselves and went to Jerusalem. Also in Judah the hand of God was on the people to give them unity of mind to carry put what the king and his officials had ordered, following the word of the LORD" (II Chronicles 30:11, 12).

As a result, "A very large crowd of people assembled in Jerusalem to celebrate the Feast of Unleavened Bread..." (II Chronicles 30:13). This was a zealous multitude. The priests and Levites had already purified the sanctuary, but the street corners were still defiled with the idolatrous altars set up by King Ahaz. In their passion for the Lord this gathering of God's children trashed those altars, throwing them into the Kidron Valley where the despicable stuff which had sullied the Temple had already been tossed. The streets of the Holy City were now emptied of unholy things. The Passover celebration was off to a promising start!

The priests and Levites were moved by the level of spiritual fervor they saw reflected in the crowd of worshipers. They felt shame over the relatively half-hearted zeal they had themselves demonstrated. They re-consecrated their lives to God and set about fulfilling their callings with fresh devotion. Following the slaughter of the Passover lamb, the priests and Levites brought burnt offerings to the Temple and worked together in obedience to the Law of God. A revival spirit had become contagious!

Essential ceremonial oversights, however, threatened to bring this glorious festival to an unhappy conclusion. Many in the assembly of worshipers from the Northern Kingdom had not purified themselves for Passover according to the Law. As a result, the Passover lambs which could not be consecrated by these ceremonially unclean worshipers were so numerous that the Levites reached beyond their divinely prescribed duties to handle the slaughter of such sacrifices. This also brought the unconsecrated Israelites in the crowd under threat of judgment for their disobedience in the matter. They should not have eaten the Passover.

Hezekiah quickly grasped the dilemma at hand. He saw the lack of conformity to the Passover regulations, but He didn't allow his vision to be shortsighted by these shortcomings. The king looked past the deficiencies to see the sincere hearts of these people. "But Hezekiah prayed for them, saying, 'May the LORD, who is good, pardon everyone who sets his heart on seeking God — the LORD, the God of his fathers — even if he is not clean according to the rules of the sanctuary.' And the LORD heard Hezekiah and healed the people" (II Chronicles 30:18-20). Godly leaders exercise mercy, knowing that the Lord is a God of mercy. Again, James 2:13 affirms: "Mercy triumphs over judgment!"

The Passover feast continued, and not as dry, empty ritual. The proceedings were jubilant and full of life. The latter part of II Chronicles chapter 30 conveys this image with phrases like: "celebrated the feast ...with great rejoicing," "sang to the LORD every day," "praised the LORD," "celebrated joyfully," "there was great joy in Jerusalem." In fact, after the allotted seven days of the feast, "the whole assembly then agreed to celebrate the festival for seven more days..." (II Chronicles 30:23). That's what a spirit of revival can do to a people hungry for more of God!

That spirit still stirred powerfully in the souls of the Jews who had participated, even after the second week had expired. II Chronicles 31 begins with the report of the ongoing effects of the faith and fervor generated by fourteen days of genuine consecration, praise, and worship of Yahweh. "When all this had ended, the Israelites who were there went out to the towns of Judah, smashed the sacred stones and cut down the Asherah poles. They destroyed the high places and the altars throughout Judah and Benjamin and in Ephraim and Manasseh. After they had destroyed all of them, the Israelites returned to their own towns and to their own property."

Hezekiah's zeal for God had helped kindle fire in thousands of his fellow Israelites. Even aliens (non-Jews) living in the land had turned to the Lord. Idolatrous images and structures were torn to the ground. The purification that had begun in the Temple had spread throughout the nation to open hearts. Revival must begin in the house of God among the people of God. It can spread from there to unbelievers throughout a nation and even around the world.

One of the characteristics of this spiritual resurgence was an atmosphere of generosity. It started with the king and his officials. The Bible narrative tells of how they contributed freely to the work of the Lord from their own personal possessions and treasuries. But liberality was not confined to finances and material goods. As already noted, the king was charitable in his mercy toward those who fell short of the standards of the Law. He was benevolent, too, in his praise and encouragement toward those who carried out their duties with devotion and diligence. Leaders should lead in all things, and Hezekiah understood this principle. He and the elders led the way in generosity, as well as in holy consecration.

Such generosity proved to be contagious. When the king sent word to his subjects that they were to restart the support of the Levites as instructed in the Law, their response was overwhelming. They brought their tithes faithfully, and the result was impressive. "When Hezekiah and his officials came and saw the heaps, they praised the LORD and blessed his people Israel" (II Chronicles 31:8). The bounty was so great that Hezekiah had to order storerooms to be prepared in the sanctuary, and assign supervisors to oversee the storage and distribution of those contributions.

Scripture sums up the fledgling sovereign's work in restoring the worship of the true God of Israel in words of commendation. "This is what Hezekiah did throughout Judah, doing what was good and right and faithful before the LORD his God. In everything that he undertook in the service of God's temple and in obedience to the law and the commands, he sought his God and worked wholeheartedly. And so he prospered" (II Chronicles 31:20,21). Sadly, that prosperity was about to fall under a dark cloud looming just beyond the horizon.

II Chronicles introduces the arrival of this momentous event in such a way that it immediately raises questions about the ways of God. "After all that Hezekiah had so faithfully done, Sennacherib king of Assyria came and invaded Judah" (II Chronicles 32:1). There's something in each of us which instinctively reacts to that statement by asking: "Is this how the Lord rewards his servants for their loyal obedience?" The answer is: yes, He often does.

Certainly Hezekiah and his people had been blessed with prosperity because of the king's faithfulness. We saw that in II Chronicles 31:21 as quoted above. Understand, however, that though one test passed is usually rewarded with God's blessings, it's also often followed by another test more difficult that the previous one. James 1:2-4 offers an explanation, and encourages a proper response. "Consider it pure joy, my brothers, whenever you face trials of many kinds, because you know that the testing of your faith develops perseverance. Perseverance must finish its work so that you may be mature and complete, not lacking anything." This pattern is part of God's plan to develop spiritual character in us.

So the king returned to the divine classroom to learn a deeper level of faith, and face a more rigorous examination than before. This episode is recorded in II Kings, II Chronicles, and Isaiah, but only II Kings gives us the story of the preliminary stage in the test when Hezekiah didn't fare so well. If he had only learned a lesson from one of his father's mistakes, he could have avoided that initial poor showing.

Instead of turning to the Lord for help when he came under attack by the Edomites and the Philistines, King Ahaz had turned to a pagan king: Tiglath-Pileser of

Assyria. In order to pay for this protection he pilfered wealth from the Temple, the palace, and the princes. It proved to be not only a costly decision, but a bad one as well. II Chronicles 28:20 states the results rather bluntly. "Tiglath-Pileser king of Assyria came to him, but he gave him trouble instead of help."

Upon ascending to the throne, Hezekiah had swiftly and righteously reversed his father's idolatry and restored the worship of Yahweh. In a time of weakness, however, he would allow the fear of men rather than the fear of the Lord to dictate how he dealt with the matter of the Assyrians. At some point during his reign Hezekiah boldly stood up and rebelled against the king of Assyria (II Kings 18:7). During the fourteenth year of his reign though, when Sennacherib, king of Assyria attacked Judah, he changed course. Hezekiah then reverted to his father's reliance on trying to buy peace and protection from men.

Much like Ahaz before him, Hezekiah tried to turn a heathen empire into a friend by buying them off. He sent word to Sennacherib: "I have done wrong. Withdraw from me, and I will pay whatever you demand of me" (II Kings 18:14). The price extracted from the Kingdom of Judah was roughly eleven tons of silver and one ton of gold. Sadly, much of that silver and gold came from the Holy Temple Hezekiah had previously restored. He even "… stripped off the gold with which he had covered the doors and doorposts of the temple of the LORD, and gave it to the king of Assyria" (II Kings 18:16).

In that moment Hezekiah would have done much better if he had drawn on the military philosophy of his ancestor King David, rather than that of his father Ahaz. David understood that the only reliable ally of the righteous was the Lord. He had learned to make prayer the foundation of his strategy in war. "Give us aid against the enemy, for the help of man is worthless. With God we will gain the victory, and he will trample down our enemies" (Psalm 60:11,12). Eventually Hezekiah would grasp this truth, and pass the remainder of the test he had begun so poorly.

The King of Assyria accepted the bounty offered by the King of Judah. The duplicitous Sennacherib then took the money and ran... not away... but to the very gates of the last bastion in Hezekiah's kingdom: the Holy City of Jerusalem! Well, actually, Sennacherib himself stayed behind at Lachish, but sent a massive army and his high ranking representatives to confront the embattled ruler and his people.

They stood outside the walls of the city and called for the king himself to appear before them. When Hezekiah sent his official agents instead, the Assyrian commander shouted out the message, ostensibly meant to be from Sennacherib to Hezekiah. It ridiculed the confidence of the Jewish sovereign, accenting his position of comparative military weakness, and arguing that he couldn't even depend on the help of Yahweh. The statement alleged that Hezekiah's removal of the idolatrous structures erected by his father Ahaz had been an affront to the God of Israel, negating any possibility of divine favor. Sennacherib even claimed that he was acting under orders from the Lord in attacking Jerusalem.

When Hezekiah's representatives asked the Assyrians to speak in Aramaic, their own diplomatic language, rather than in Hebrew, the ruse of this being a personal communiqué from Sennacherib to Hezekiah was exposed. They had spoken publicly in Hebrew because the message was meant for the population at large to hear, in an effort to create fear and undermine their confidence in the Lord and their king. The enemy commander responded: "Was it only to your master and you that my master sent me to say these things, and not to the men sitting on the wall — who, like you, will have to eat their own filth and drink their own urine?" (II Kings 18:27).

The rantings of Sennacherib's field commander continued, at this point with no pretense of it being a personal message between rulers. He scorned Hezekiah's assurances to his subjects that God would deliver Jerusalem, instead offering them false promises of prosperity in another land if they surrendered to him. His words then turned blasphemous, comparing the God of Israel to the false gods of other nations conquered by the Assyrians. "Who of all the gods of these countries has been able to save his land from me? How then can the LORD deliver Jerusalem from my hand?" (I Kings 18:35).

Hezekiah's officials tore their clothes in outraged response to these insults, grieving over such a distressing situation. The king himself reacted in much the same way when they passed the message along to him. He tore his clothes, put on sackcloth garments indicative of mourning, and headed for the Temple to seek the Lord. He also sent word of what had happened to God's faithful prophet, Isaiah, asking the man of God to pray.

Isaiah was a man whose spirit was sensitive to the voice of the Lord, and his reply to the king was prompt. His words were not his own, they were from the lips of Yahweh Himself and meant to dispel fear. "Do not be afraid of what you have heard — those words with which the underlings of the king of Assyria have blasphemed me" (II Kings

19:6). God went on to proclaim that He would intervene and cause Sennacherib to return home, where he would subsequently pay for his insolence with his life.

If based on Isaiah's prophecy Hezekiah had expected an instant deliverance, he would have been very much disappointed. As is many times the case, the Word of the Lord did not come to pass immediately. I'm reminded of the reference to the necessity of waiting on the Lord's timing found in Hebrews 6:12. There God urges His people "to imitate those who through faith and patience inherit what has been promised." We need to hold on in faith even when our circumstances scream that the Lord has forgotten his promises.

While initially it may have *appeared* that fulfillment of the prophecy concerning Sennacherib's return to his native land was imminent, it was not to be. A few verses after the promise of God's intervention, Hezekiah's hopes may have been raised by events that seemed suggestive of part of Isaiah's prophecy. Perhaps now the time of deliverance was at hand. Not so. Instead the enemy sent yet another blasphemous correspondence to Judah's king, insisting that the God of Israel could not prevent the fall of the Holy City.

Once more Hezekiah made his way to the sanctuary. This time however, he forwarded no prayer request to Isaiah. He spread the troubling letter before the Lord and he himself cried out to God. This supplication, recorded in II Kings 19:15-19, was more concerned with the honor of the Lord than anything else. He asked for victory against the enemy, but his priority was the glory of God. He lamented the insults hurled at Yahweh. His intercession ended with this appeal: "Now, O LORD our God, deliver us from his hand, so that all kingdoms on earth may know that you alone, O LORD, are God."

A second time Isaiah heard from the Lord about the Assyrian menace, and this time the prophetic word was more expansive. Isaiah passed it along to Hezekiah. You can read the full text in II Kings 19:21-28 or Isaiah 37:22-29. In it God mocked Sennacherib's arrogance, reminding him that his authority and previous success had been ordained by the Almighty Who rules from heaven and sets up and deposes earthly rulers as He wills. The Lord declared that He had heard the Assyrian monarch's blasphemy against "the Holy One of Israel" and would dictate his return to his home in Nineveh, where as He had earlier declared, Sennacherib would be "cut down with the sword."

A further encouraging prophecy was directed to Hezekiah. It's found in II Kings 19:29-34 and Isaiah 37:30-35. In it the Lord promised restoration and prosperity for the survivors in the Kingdom of Judah, and decreed that the king of Assyria would never "enter this city or shoot an arrow here." No Israeli soldier would need to raise a sword in battle. God Himself would defend Jerusalem! Hezekiah would have to wait a while for the predicted death of Sennacherib, but the divine deliverance of the city would almost immediately come thundering down like an unexpected bolt of lightning from the heavens.

"That night the angel of the LORD went out and put to death a hundred and eighty-five thousand men in the Assyrian camp. When the people got up the next morning — there were all the dead bodies!" (II Kings 19:35). The suddenness of this divine judgment appears to have come as a shock to the children of God. Occasionally that happens. Our Heavenly Father is always faithful to His promises and His people. Frequently answers to prayers take time... even *much* time. Now and then they come without delay. In His wisdom the Lord establishes the timetable. Those who learn the lessons of Biblical faith will hold on through the toughest trials and trust God's infallible perspective.

Oh... and the death of Sennacherib back home in his capitol prophesied by Isaiah? "So Sennacherib king of Assyria broke camp and withdrew. He returned to Nineveh and stayed there. One day, while he was worshiping in the temple of his god Nisroch, his sons Adrammelech and Sharezer cut him down with the sword..." (II Kings 19:36, 37). That's the end of the story, right? Not quite. There are two more important documented incidents in Hezekiah's life connected to the Assyrian menace. Both of them will show us a side of the king we've not seen before.

A critical illness is mentioned in all three accounts of Hezekiah's life, but II Kings and Isaiah provide more extensive coverage. II Kings 20:1 begins the story by establishing the historical context: "In those days..." Since they immediately follow the story of the Assyrian invasion, these words would seem to indicate that Hezekiah's sickness occurred at some point during that military crisis. Simple arithmetic confirms it. Hezekiah reigned for 29 years. When God sent word that he would heal the king, He promised to extend his life by 15 years. That places this event in the 14th year of his reign, the same year of Sennacherib's invasion. The precise moment is unknown, but the general time frame is supplied.

Whatever sickness descended upon the king eventually became terminal. Scripture identifies it as a boil. However, the Hebrew word used there can refer not only to a boil, but to other skin diseases involving inflammation and/or infection. Whatever the specifics, Hezekiah drew near to death. Isaiah the prophet brought him a message from God that he would die from the illness and that he should get his house in order. This turn of events may prompt us to ask the age old question: Why do bad things happen to good people? That question certainly arose in the ailing ruler's mind.

Hezekiah's reaction to his painful circumstances affords us insight into character flaws that heretofore had remained overshadowed by his godly traits. These new features result in a less complimentary portrait of the man than we might have at first expected. He "turned his face to the wall" (II Kings 20:2) and prayed a rather self-centered prayer. "'Remember, O LORD, how I have walked before you faithfully and with wholehearted devotion and have done what is good in your eyes.' And Hezekiah wept bitterly" (II Kings 20:3). The overall depiction is that of a sulking adolescent. In fact, the same Hebrew phrasing found in verse 2 is translated as "sulking" in reference to wicked king Ahab of Samaria in I Kings 21:4.

Isaiah's recounting of the king's later journal of the event provides a further peek into his fairly egocentric attitude at the time. "I said 'In the prime of my life must I go through the gates of death and be robbed of the rest of my years?'" (Isaiah 38:10). The use of the word "robbed" here indicates Hezekiah's sense of entitlement about his life. Could it be that we possess that same mind-set? Are our lives our own, or do they belong to the Lord?

What we see now is self-righteousness. Hezekiah was essentially a good man, but even the best among us have no inherent claim on God's goodness. "Because of the LORD's great love we are not consumed, for his compassions never fail" (Lamentations 3:22). Does God honor human faithfulness? Yes. But His goodness only flows through His love, mercy, and grace. "...for all have sinned and fall short of the glory of God" (Romans 3:23). Hezekiah was misguided in thinking that his own good deeds qualified him to receive healing from the Lord.

Despite Hezekiah's shortcomings, God chose to respond favorably to his pleas. The Lord caught Isaiah on his way out of the palace and sent him back with the good news. "...I have heard your prayer and seen your tears; I will heal you..." (II Kings 20:5). Besides the promises relating to the king's healing and added years of life, Yahweh addressed the military dilemma facing Hezekiah and his people. "And I will deliver you and this city from the hand of the king of Assyria. I will defend this city for my sake and for the sake of my servant David" (II Kings 20:6).

At the king's request, God even gave him a miraculous sign of His promise that he would be so completely healed in three days that he would go up to the Temple (II Kings 20:5). Offered the choice of the shadow on the stairway of Ahaz going forward ten steps or backward ten steps, Hezekiah chose the latter sign since it would be a more clearly supernatural event. The Lord did just that, and Hekekiah's health was restored.

As a bit of an aside let me call attention to another truth found in this story, one illustrated by the means which God used to heal Hezekiah. Through His prophet God commanded a poultice of figs to be prepared and applied to the boil. He could have had Isaiah pray over the king, perhaps laying hands on him, and then supernaturally cured him. Instead, the Lord used medicine from the material world to heal Hezekiah.

I have never forgotten the words I heard spoken many years ago by a man of God. He reminded us: "Jesus walked on the water. Most of the time He took the boat." The preacher's point was both simple and profound. Those rather obvious truths from Scripture sometimes escape us. Should He choose, the Lord's provision for His children could flow miraculously to them in *every* time of need. Still, He *frequently* uses earthly means to meet our needs... including boats! Healing can come through God's supernatural power, or through conventional and natural medicine.

Though II Chronicles devotes only a single sentence (II Chronicles 32:24) to Hezekiah's sickness and healing, it does go on to share important information left out in II Kings and Isaiah. "But Hezekiah's heart was proud and he did not respond to the kindness shown him; therefore the Lord's wrath was on him and on Judah and Jerusalem. Then Hezekiah repented of the pride of his heart, as did the people of Jerusalem; therefore the Lord's wrath did not come upon them during the days of Hezekiah" (II Chronicles 32:25,26).

Evidently, in the wake of his illness and subsequent healing from the Lord, pride rose up as in Hezekiah's heart, a pride that spread to his subjects. We suspect it may have been a misguided response to God healing the king of his terminal illness. We mortals are often inclined to react to God's gracious interventions that way, thinking that His favor is bestowed simply because of our own goodness. In any event, the anger of the Almighty over this ungodly conceit could have led to great judgment for Hezekiah and his people. Thankfully, however, the ruler and his capitol city were spared from chastisement when they repented of their sin. The Lord is merciful, and when Hezekiah and his people repented of their pride, He withheld His judgment.

Hezekiah eventually recognized his pride problem and determined to overcome it. The king's post-healing reflection on his experience is recorded in Isaiah. He clearly understood that God had allowed his ordeal to teach him some things. "Surely it was for my benefit that I suffered such anguish" (Isaiah 38:17). He resolved to bury his sinful vanity. "I will walk humbly all my years because of this anguish of my soul" (Isaiah 38:15). Pride is indeed a sly enemy of godliness, a foe which, with the help of the Lord, we must frequently battle.

My mind goes back to an evening in the summer of 1967. I was 18 years old. I had graduated from high school and would be headed off to Bible school in the fall. I had attended a youth rally in Newcastle, Pennsylvania and at the close of the service had gone to the altar to spend some time in prayer. While seeking the Lord I acknowledged my many shortcomings and sincerely confessed them to Him. I poured out my heart and told him what a wretch I was, asking for His forgiveness and His help to become more like Jesus.

My prayers were born of genuine conviction and humbled me before God. I rose from my knees and headed toward the foyer of the church to prepare for the ride home. Without thinking... in an instant... I began figuratively patting myself on the back. "You're a good man, Sam Mason. Not many Christians would have enough humility to admit all their faults to the Lord like that!"

What had happened? Had my confessions been hypocritical? No. The self-effacing supplications had come from my heart. But pride is a subtle and devious sin. Stomp it down with all of your might and it will squeeze back up from between your toes. We'll in due course learn that periodic rumors of its final demise are greatly exaggerated. Pride is one of those nagging sins which must be fought to one degree or another for a lifetime. If we fervently pursue God's help we'll advance toward ultimate victory, but we, like Hezekiah, must always be on our guard against it.

There is yet a final key event from the reign of Hezekiah which we must scrutinize. It also happens to be the story most pertinent to the primary subject at hand. All three books narrating the life of Hezekiah record this episode, but only one of them logs the unusual aspect that arrests our attention and demands a closer look. Although II Kings chapter 20 and Isaiah chapter 39 also refer to this affair, only II Chronicles chapter 32, precedes the mention of it with a litany of the king's numerous accomplishments and many possessions in verses 27 through 30. Reviewing these achievements could be an appropriate precursor to a flare-up of Hezekiah's pride problem.

Hezekiah's recovery from a terminal illness, and the accompanying supernatural sign of the sun moving backward, had captivated the minds of others in that part of the world... including the rulers of an emerging superpower. The Babylonians dispatched envoys to Jerusalem with favorable correspondence and a gift for the king of Judah. They wanted to know more about how and why the sun had suddenly reversed course. This could have been a grand opportunity for Hezekiah to speak of the goodness and power of the one true God of the universe.

Sadly, it seems that he chose to make it an occasion to show off his wealth. Hezekiah's nemesis had stepped into the spotlight. Pride provoked him to lead the Babylonian emissaries on an exhaustive tour of his treasures. So thorough was this tour that II Kings 20:13 sums it up by declaring "There was nothing in his palace or in all his kingdom that Hezekiah did not show them." Could this prideful action be connected to the aforementioned episode recorded in II Chronicles 32:25, 26? Or is it yet an additional instance of egotism rearing it's ugly head?

Further understanding the king's disappointing behavior begins with reading II Chronicles 32:31. It renders additional insight into the problem of pride in the hearts of God's servants, and how the Lord may choose to deal with it. "But when envoys were sent by the rulers of Babylon to ask him about the miraculous sign that had occurred in the land, God left him to test him and know everything that was in his heart." An exalted view of ourselves can lead to dark days, spiritually speaking. For a season the Presence of God departed from Hezekiah!

The statement in II Chronicles 32:31 of the Lord's purpose in leaving Hezekiah, "to test him and know everything that was in his heart," is strikingly similar to a passage in Deuteronomy 8:2. At the end of Israel's four decades of wilderness wanderings, Moses had been reviewing their journey and the lessons to be learned from it. "Remember how the LORD your God led you all the way in the desert these forty years, to humble you and

to test you in order to know what was in your heart..."
Just as the Sinai wilderness had humbled and tested the
wandering Israelites centuries earlier, the wilderness of
estrangement from God's Presence would now humble
and test Hezekiah.

How desperately we need the Presence of the Lord
to be active in our lives if we're to live righteously! There
is a raging conflict within each of us that cannot be won
in our own strength, no matter how intense our personal
resolve. The Apostle Paul enlightened us on this matter in
Galatians 5:16, 17. "So I say, live by the Spirit, and you will
not gratify the desires of the sinful nature. For the sinful
nature desires what is contrary to the Spirit, and the Spirit
what is contrary to the sinful nature. They are in conflict
with each other, so that you do not do what you want."

Hezekiah had intended to walk in humility the rest of
his life. He was the sovereign ruler of God's people. He
commanded and his servants and subjects obeyed. He
knew how to maintain control. Surely *he* could win this war
against the sin of pride! He'd been the most godly king in
the history of Judah. He had honored the Lord in so many
ways during his reign. It may have seemed to the king that
he had overcome pride, but the omniscient Creator knew
better. Yahweh had already recognized the weakness
within Hezekiah. It was not for God's benefit that the
contents of the king's heart needed to be revealed... it
was for the Hezekiah's own good!

We're often dangerously slow to understand the
wicked potential that resides in our old sinful nature. We
may think that at some point we have it under control, but
we're just fooling ourselves. Only the powerful Presence
of the Holy Spirit can enable us to live in victory. We never

outgrow our need for Him. Our walk with God is a lifetime of dependence on the Divine Presence, and the sooner we grasp that fact, the better! The Lord had to leave Hezekiah to his own devices... removing His Manifest Presence for a season... if there were to be any hope that the king would learn this vital truth.

We're not told how long the test lasted, but the conversations between Isaiah and Hezekiah which ensued suggest it took an extended time for this essential principle to sink in. The prophet asked the ruler about the visitors from Babylon. What did they say? Where did they come from? What did they see in his palace? Hezekiah's answers pleased neither the Lord nor his prophet. "They came from Babylon" (II Kings 20:14). "They saw everything in my palace... There is nothing among my treasures that I did not show them" (II Kings 20:15). The king's naiveté and self-satisfaction were evident.

Isaiah's anointed retort was a rebuke that seemed not to fully register with Hezekiah. Everything that generations of Jewish royalty had accumulated would at a future date be carried off to Babylon, and some of the king's descendents would become eunuchs in the Babylonian palace. Hezekiah's reaction? "The word of the LORD you have spoken is good," Hezekiah replied. For he thought, "Will there not be peace and security in my lifetime?" (II Kings 20:19). Such reasoning smacks of preoccupation with self absorption. Those are the last words of Hezekiah recorded in the Bible. In the years ahead did he fully grasp the truths about the dangers of pride that God wanted him to learn? We can only hope so.

Lest we judge Hezekiah too harshly, let me remind you of God's assessment of him quoted early in this chapter.

"Hezekiah trusted in the LORD, the God of Israel. There was no one like him among all the kings of Judah, either before him or after him. He held fast to the LORD and did not cease to follow him; he kept the commands the LORD had given Moses" (II Kings 18:5, 6). As the account of his life drew to a close, the inspired author of II Chronicles reminded us of "his acts of devotion," and concluded by telling us "All Judah and the people of Jerusalem honored him when he died."

We have to acknowledge Hezekiah's skirmishes with pride. He sometimes allowed his good deeds, and the blessings and prosperity that resulted from them, to go to his head. Even the finest among believers are flawed. The story of Hezekiah, son of Ahaz, has reminded us of that, and other helpful Bible truths. Our spiritual education has been advanced by the study of his life. Let's take a few moments now to look back on some of the most important lessons we can extract from it.

Lesson 1: A bad environment is no excuse for bad character. Hezekiah was brought up by a wicked father, in an idolatrous society. Yet he developed a heart for the Lord in the midst of such iniquity. From the time the reins of the kingdom were placed in his young hands he began to lead his people back to God. Would we like to see every child brought up in a Christian home and taken faithfully to the House of God? Absolutely! Even in godless surroundings however, there is a God -given conscience that declares what is right and what is wrong, and an ingrained longing for the God Who is real. Each one of us must decide for ourselves who we will follow and how we will live.

Lesson 2: Spiritual revival is the most essential need in a declining nation. No otherwise beneficial political movement can long prevail in a land which has rejected God and His Word. Hezekiah's civil reforms and civic and national defense improvements were delayed while calling the nation back to the Lord. God give us governmental leaders who understand and implement such priorities! In a nation like America, may Christians set the example, then prayerfully guided by these values, vote to elect God-fearing leaders!

Lesson 3: Unholy alliances lead to trouble. Faith in the Lord can deliver us. Hezekiah's father, Ahaz, had established an unrighteous union with the king of the pagan empire of Assyria in a time of crisis. Early in his leadership Hezekiah virtuously stood against this previously generated pact. But when Assyria attacked, he chose to surrender to earthly fear rather than trust God, paying a high price in a futile effort to ransom Judah from the enemy's bullying. Fortunately, in the end Hezekiah reached out to Yahweh in faith and experienced the resounding victory that comes from fully trusting the Lord.

Like Hezekiah, we're often inclined to surrender to fear and yield to the demands of our enemy: the old, sinful nature. We think that satisfying its desires will bring peace. But peace is not the product of surrender to an unholy adversary. It's the fruit of the prayer of faith. "Do not be anxious about anything, but in everything, by prayer and petition, with thanksgiving, present your requests to God. And the peace of God, which transcends all understanding, will guard your hearts and your minds in Christ Jesus" (Philippians 4:6, 7).

Lesson 4: Even the most godly among us wrestle with pride. It was not mere men who spoke highly of Hezekiah's character. It was God Himself Who declared him so special in His eyes. We witnessed the king's wholesome desires and deeds as we studied his history. His latent self-absorption and pride, however, also rose to the surface at times and revealed themselves in the pages of Scripture. None of us are exempt from such temptation. It's so easy for the old nature to derive a sense of self-importance from the admirable acts of the new nature and the mercy of God.

We must recognize with the Apostle Paul a humbling fact of life. "I know that nothing good lives in me, that is, in my sinful nature" (Romans 7:18). He further warns all of us: "Do not think of yourself more highly than you ought..." (Romans 12:3). We have to constantly remind ourselves that any good which comes from our lives arises from the Presence of the Lord within and without. Otherwise it will go to our heads. We should walk in humility and dependence on God. If not, our self-righteousness smugness will dishonor Him, hurt those around us, and lure us away from the ways of the Lord. Never think you've spiritually arrived and are immune to the appeal of pride. Always guard your heart against it.

Lesson 5: Sometimes God must remove His Manifest Presence from us for a season in order to open our eyes to the impotence of our human condition. It's important that we examine the context of this experience in Hezekiah's life. The four verses preceding the divine departure recorded in II Chronicles 32:31 list the riches and accomplishments which had flowed to him from the Lord over the years. God had even recently healed a fatal illness and given him an amazing supernatural sign in the process. Royal envoys arrived from a distant land to inquire about such astounding events. Hezekiah began to think all these blessings were the result of his own righteousness. He needed to be reminded that he was nothing without the Lord!

Could it be that similar circumstances have happened to us? We may wonder why something seems to be missing in our spiritual lives. Perhaps God has left us for a time to test us and reveal an ugly truth lurking in the dark shadows of our hearts... a self-exalting independent streak that would steal his glory and attribute His blessings to our own supposed goodness. Maybe the missing Presence of the Lord is calling our attention to the need to get back to reliance on faith in the Living God. If you're wondering about it now, ask Him to speak to your heart. If it's so, come before Him in humble repentance. He will forgive you and restore His sweet Presence!

CHAPTER 4

A HIGHER PURPOSE

We don't usually think of Jesus as having *friends* in the common sense of the word. After all, He was God in flesh. How could a mere human being really be His friend? Those around Him were classified as followers, servants, disciples, and apostles... but friends? It's difficult for us to imagine Jesus having friends in the same way as we do. Yet He Himself made it a point to call those near and dear to Him friends. "...I have called you friends, for everything that I learned from my Father I have made known to you" (John 15:15).

Among His friends during his earthly ministry were three siblings in the village of Bethany, just outside the holy city of Jerusalem. Their names were Mary, Martha, and Lazarus. Just how dear these friends were to Him is established by what is said in John 11:5: "Jesus loved Martha and her sister and Lazarus."

Scripture provides nothing definitive about their extended family, although reading between the lines in one of the gospel accounts involving them has led to a bit of speculation on the matter. Based primarily upon the fact that Matthew chapter 26 and Mark chapter 14 indicate that a feast similar to the one recorded in John chapter 12, with the two sisters and their brother in attendance, took place in the home of Simon the leper, some believe they were his offspring. This, however, is only an assumption.

There's no information in the Gospels about the existence of any spouses or children of Mary, Martha, or Lazarus. Perhaps they were all unmarried during the time of Jesus. There does seem to be a good possibility that they resided together in the family home. At the least, we do know that they lived in the same little community, and as their story unfolds we'll see clearly that these three were bound by a deep familial love. That being said, let's explore what else we can learn from the Biblical record about this trio.

We first meet this special family in Luke 10:38-42. There we find the first of two accounts of hospitality extended to Jesus in their home. Before we look at those verses however, we need to read some instructions listed earlier in that same chapter. The Lord gave his disciples pertinent directives before sending them out into the spiritual harvest fields. A particular portion of these instructions will afford us better appreciation of the nature of Christian hospitality and the role it played in the development of the friendship between the Master and this family.

Here's what Jesus said in Luke 10:5-7: "When you enter a house, first say, 'Peace to this house.' If a man of peace is there, your peace will rest on him; if not, it will return to you. Stay in that house, eating and drinking whatever they give you, for the worker deserves his wages. Do not move around from house to house."

From the above passage we learn several principles practiced by Christ, and passed along to His disciples. First, we are to offer peace to those who open their homes and hearts to us. This is a blessing given to those who generously furnish hospitality to God's servants. If their hearts are right, this peace will remain with them. If not, it will come back to us. Hospitality is valued in any age and culture, but in ancient times in the Near East it was especially important. Such importance was intensified further by the vital message those who were sent out by the Savior carried with them.

Another principle communicated here is that long-term relationships are to be cultivated and treasured. Jesus told his disciples not to move around from house to house in each area, but to stay where they were welcomed and develop enduring friendships with their hosts. Throughout our lives and ministries we'll meet many whom we will touch, and many who will touch us. Some of those encounters will involve relatively brief passing moments, but others will become rich lifetime friendships. These are key relationships.

Finally, we come to understand that contributing to the needs of the Lord's servants is fitting. "...The worker deserves his wages" (Luke 10:7). It's an honorable thing to work for the Lord, and an honorable thing to support those who do so. There is no shame in receiving compensation as a result of efforts for the Kingdom of God. That's not to suggest that those who serve Him should take such contributions for granted or become greedy. It simply says that it's the responsibility of all God's children to support those who work for Him.

With these truths in mind, let's see what we can learn about Jesus' cherished friends in this brief story at the close of Luke chapter 10. "As Jesus and his disciples were on their way, he came to a village where a woman named Martha opened her home to him. She had a sister called Mary, who sat at the Lord's feet listening to what he said. But Martha was distracted by all the preparations that had to be made. She came to him and asked, 'Lord, don't you care that my sister has left me to do the work by myself? Tell her to help me!' 'Martha, Martha,' the Lord answered, 'you are worried and upset about many things, but only one thing is needed. Mary has chosen what is better, and it will not be taken away from her.'"

There's no mention of Lazarus at this point, so the insights we gain are about his sisters. First, let me call attention to the fact that the account refers to the home as Martha's. While it may be that that this house belonged to all three siblings and was referred to as Martha's simply because she was the one who extended the invitation and made the preparations, some scholars believe Martha may have been appointed household manager by her father. As previously noted, these learned men believe that the father of Mary, Martha, and Lazarus was "Simon the leper."

In any case, the idea of Martha as household manager would certainly be in keeping with the image of her presented in the narrative. Martha appears to be a hard-working, take-charge individual. All of us are born with inherent temperamental gifts, and as I read of Martha's words and actions in the account here in Luke 10, my mind quickly goes to a list of these kinds of gifts expounded in Romans 12. Specifically, I see Martha as one with the gift of leadership/administration (Romans 12:8), and likely the gift of serving (Romans 12:7) as well. She was busy with the efforts in which any good hostess would be engaged. Yet something was wrong. Martha was disturbed.

The source of this industrious lady's distress was both internal and external. The external irritation was situated in close proximity to the Master Himself. Martha's sister, Mary, sat at the feet of Jesus, entranced by the powerful words He spoke, while Martha labored hard at things she felt must be done to properly care for her guests. The primary source of the disturbance, however, lay within. "But Martha was distracted by all the preparations that had to be made (Luke 10:40a). So often when we lose the peace of God in our lives, it's not simply the result of circumstances, but of our attitudes.

Martha *had had it!* "She came to him (Jesus) and asked, 'Lord, don't you care that my sister has left me to do the work by myself? Tell her to help me!'" (Luke 10:40b). Now we discover that Martha was not only angry at her sister for her laziness, she was upset with Jesus for allowing Mary to get away with it! She viewed Mary as the slacker and Christ as her enabler. Though couched as a question, at the core her words were an accusation aimed at the Master. In Martha's mind He was either woefully ignorant of what was happening, or simply didn't care! It just wasn't fair!

He Who rightly judges the thoughts and deeds of all humanity quickly cut to the chase with Martha. The weight of the counsel He was about to offer was foreshadowed by his repetition of her name: "Martha, Martha..." He wanted her full attention, just as He did later with Simon Peter in Luke 22:31,32 when he warned his often overly confident disciple: "Simon, Simon, Satan has asked to sift you as wheat. But I have prayed for you, Simon, that your faith may not fail. And when you have turned back, strengthen your brothers." When the Lord speaks with such impetus, we must pay close attention.

"'Martha, Martha,' the Lord answered, 'you are worried and upset about many things, but only one thing is needed. Mary has chosen what is better, and it will not be taken away from her'" (Luke 10:41,42). Did she turn away in anger, feeling she'd been misunderstood? Or did her cheeks glow crimson in shame for her misguided attitude? We're not told her immediate reaction, but given her relationship with the Savior I'm confident that sooner or later she learned the lesson.

Make no mistake, Christ was not rebuking her for her use of the gifts of administration and service which God Himself had given her. Jesus had urged his disciples to devote themselves to the noble cause of service to others. In Mark 10:43-45 He instructed them: "...whoever wants to become great among you must be your servant, and whoever wants to be first must be slave of all. For even the Son of Man did not come to be served, but to serve, and to give his life as a ransom for many."

No, it was not her *use* of her gifts, but her *misuse* of them that concerned Him. Our natural gifts carry great potential for good, but our fallen nature inclines them toward abuse and imbalance. Thus godly priorities can be thrown into disorder. That's what happened to Martha in this instance.

Many years ago I listened as a seasoned servant of God made a sage observation. "Sometimes we get so involved in the work of the Lord that we neglect the Lord of the work." That's a valuable insight. Many of us have struggled with just such a spiritual imbalance. The Biblical record of this incident marks Martha as a prominent historical member of that imprudent society.

We ought not react to this episode by thinking of Martha as a bad person. That was not the implication Christ intended. Bear in mind that she had graciously and generously opened her home and offered of her substance to care for the Master and his disciples. That was a righteous endeavor. Her shortcoming was in allowing her *labor for* the Lord to take precedence over her *intimacy with* the Lord, and subsequently foster hurt and anger. Some theologians believe that the fault initially lay in the lavish degree of Martha's preparations. They suggest she would have been better served by keeping things simple, allowing her to spend more personal time with Jesus.

Whatever the details behind the event, it was clearly a matter of the *good* victimizing the *best*. Martha focused on her labors for the Lord, while Mary concentrated on the Lord Himself and His words. As a consequence, Martha received correction, whereas Mary was commended.

Let's take a closer look at Mary's part in this drama. At first glance, it might seem that Martha was justified in her irritation at her sister. Martha worked while Mary sat. Martha grumbled: "...my sister has left me to do the work by myself." The wording in the original Greek suggests that Mary may have spent some time assisting Martha, but eventually left before the preparations were complete. We're not certain of all the details involved. Still, it's easy to see the situation through Martha's eyes. We may even identify with Martha's complaint.

Jesus, however, saw things much differently. That's why it's so important that we leave final judgment in such matters to the Lord Himself. Human understanding is flawed and easily misled. We should seek to view people and events from God's perspective.

The Son of God knew that His Father had taught His children "...that man does not live on bread alone but on every word that comes from the mouth of the LORD" (Deuteronomy 8:3b). Christ had even quoted this Scripture passage as a rebuke to Satan during His wilderness temptations. Was the feast Martha was preparing a good and useful thing? Of course it was. Yet there is a hunger more vital than that for *physical* nourishment. Mary was pursuing essential *spiritual* food.

Through His intimacy with the Father, Jesus instinctively lived out this principle. An incident chronicled in the 4th chapter of the Gospel of John illustrates it well. He and His disciples had been traveling through Samaria. Weary from the journey, Christ sat down by Jacob's well while His disciples headed for the nearby town of Sychar to buy food. There transpired the familiar story of His life-changing conversation with the woman at the well. A remarkable revival was the ultimate result of that blessed discussion!

The part of the account most pertinent to the subject at hand, however, occurs after the disciples returned from town with food and urged the Master to eat. "But he said to them, 'I have food to eat that you know nothing about.' Then his disciples said to each other, 'Could someone have brought him food?' 'My food,' said Jesus, 'is to do the will of him who sent me and to finish his work'" (John 4:32-34).

Jesus had satisfied his spiritual hunger by doing the will of God. He understood that both the discovery and the implementation of God's will begins with an open heart and an open ear, while enjoying sweet fellowship with the Father. The Gospels document his lifestyle of regular periods of extended time alone with God, praying and listening. Like her Savior, Mary too had been feeding her spirit and engaging in the highest will of God by sitting at the feet of Jesus and absorbing His words.

This is the most essential activity in the life of each believer. Martha was distracted by her external responsibilities and had lost the peace of God. Mary was enveloped in the peace of God as she sat at the feet of Jesus. The Lord saw Martha's condition, and as previously noted, advised her accordingly. "...Only one thing is needed. Mary has chosen what is better, and it will not be taken away from her." Nothing is more important in the life of every Christian than spending time in His Presence, feeding on His Word. Whatever aspect of the work of the Lord in which we're engaged, we must keep the main thing, the main thing! This truth is even more fundamental for those who are called to preach and teach.

A problem which arose in the Early Church shines some light on the issue. "In those days when the number of disciples was increasing, the Grecian Jews among them complained against the Hebraic Jews because their widows were being overlooked in the daily distribution of food. So the Twelve gathered all the disciples together and said, 'It would not be right for us to neglect the ministry of the word of God in order to wait on tables. Brothers, choose seven men from among you who are known to be full of the Spirit and wisdom. We will turn this responsibility over to them and will give our attention to prayer and the ministry of the word'" (Acts 6:1-4). Preachers and teachers take note! Time in prayer and the Word must be given precedence over all other godly activity.

Singer and songwriter Larnelle Harris captured the indispensable nature of those periods in prayer and the Word in a song titled: "I Miss My Time with You." The chorus is written from the perspective of the Lord Himself as He laments the loss of regular intimate communion with His otherwise preoccupied servant.

> I miss my time with you, those
> moments together.
> I need to be with you each day,
> and it hurts Me when you say
> You're too busy, busy trying to serve Me.
> But how can you serve Me
> when your spirit's empty?
> There's a longing in my heart, wanting
> more than just a part of you.
> It's true, I miss My time with you.

I hope those lyrics help to bring home to you the importance of the primary message of the story we've just examined.

So what have we learned about the sisters from the closing verses of Luke chapter 10? We see that they were both God-fearing women who were determined to follow and serve the Lord Jesus. Each, however, possessed a distinct temperament and unique gifts. On this particular occasion, Martha had allowed her gifts to get in the way of her deepest spiritual needs and responsibilities. Mary, on the other hand, had taken advantage of an opportunity to demonstrate her devotion to the Master by sitting at His feet and soaking it all in. Mary had chosen what is better.

An excerpt from yet another song may help us apply what we've just learned to our own lives. "Lo! I Come with Joy to Do" was written centuries ago by Charles Wesley. Still, it's balanced truth resonates in our spirits today:

> Faithful to my Lord's commands,
> I still would choose the better part;
> Serve with careful Martha's hands,
> and loving Mary's heart.

These images of Mary and Martha are reinforced and deepened by another event chronicled in John 12:1-8. This affair occurred after the pivotal raising of Lazarus from the dead, an event we'll investigate more fully later in this chapter. In the wake of that miracle, many more had come to faith in Christ. As a result, the chief priests and Pharisees, who opposed Jesus, had determined to kill Him. He and His disciples subsequently withdrew from Jerusalem to the village of Ephraim, near the desert, and refrained from public appearances in the Holy City for a time.

The Passover celebration was near, and in spite of the plot against His life, Jesus planned to return to Jerusalem to observe it with His followers. He also understood that His sacrificial death for the sins of all mankind would soon take place there. A week before the Passover, He set out for Bethany, the hometown of Mary, Martha, and Lazarus, which was in close proximity to Jerusalem. There a meal was prepared in honor of the Master. Perhaps it was in celebration of Lazarus' resurrection. It featured Martha serving as we would expect. Martha was an organizer and a servant at heart. Lazarus, meanwhile, "was among those reclining at the table" with Christ.

A short time later their sister moved to center stage in this scene. "Then Mary took about a pint of pure nard, an expensive perfume; she poured it on Jesus' feet and wiped his feet with her hair. And the house was filled with the fragrance of the perfume" (John 12:3). Whatever the quantity, the spikenard she used would have been considered an extravagant expenditure. It was a highly prized and extremely expensive perfume created from a plant grown in faraway northern India. The pint she lavished on the Savior would have cost a year's wages!

To Jesus this spoke of her lavish devotion to God and His Son. Judas Iscariot, however, saw it otherwise: ""Why wasn't this perfume sold and the money given to the poor? It was worth a year's wages" (John 12:5). At the least, he was accusing Mary of misplaced priorities. We might view Judas' concern as reasonable, perhaps even noble, had the Bible not revealed His true motives. "He did not say this because he cared about the poor but because he was a thief; as keeper of the money bag, he used to help himself to what was put into it" (John 12:6). When the sweet fragrance of true worship fills the room, most believers are enthralled by it and drawn to it, but in Judas this scent provoked greed and judgmentalism.

We're left to speculate about Mary's reaction to this harsh criticism. One of Jesus' close circle of twelve disciples (indeed, His treasurer!) had accused her of reckless extravagance and callousness toward the less fortunate. Such a stern indictment in front of family and friends likely stung her. Chances are her tender spirit was deeply wounded. Have you ever been there? Have you done something with good intentions… only to receive an unkind rebuke as your reward?

Christ was quick to come to Mary's defense, providing divine perspective on the issue at hand. "'Leave her alone,' Jesus replied. 'It was intended that she should save this perfume for the day of my burial. You will always have the poor among you, but you will not always have me'" (John 12:7,8). The Lord was saying that Mary's deed was not only a good one, it was *ordained by God!* Whether she was conscious of it or not, she was anointing Him for His burial… just days away. Mary had not been ignoring the needs of the poor, she had been ministering to the Lord Himself! Remember, loving our neighbor is the *second greatest* commandment. The *supreme* commandment is to love the Lord with all our being.

We must not be quick to criticize the actions of others. Only God fully knows the heart. Only He will be the final judge of all. It's His approbation we should seek, not that of fellow humans.

Many years ago I stood in church during the after service on a Sunday evening. I was feeling discouraged. I lamented my concerns to the Lord. There were key people in my life and ministry whom I felt I was not making happy. This troubled me. I concluded by confessing that I was even disappointing myself! When my prayer was done, deep in my spirit I clearly heard God speak two words: "Please Me." I needed to be less concerned about satisfying people and more focused on satisfying my Master. Pleasing the Lord does not necessarily result in pleasing people, and vice-versa. My priority is to bring joy to the heart of the Lord by what I do. Decades later that lesson still lingers in my mind.

IF ONLY I KNEW WHERE TO FIND HIM!

To Jesus, Mary's act of devotion spoke of His impending death for mankind. The closing commentary on this story tells us that it also threatened the death of Mary's brother. Lazarus' recent resurrection (which we'll discuss more fully momentarily) was painting a bulls eye on his back. "Meanwhile a large crowd of Jews found out that Jesus was there and came, not only because of him but also to see Lazarus, whom he had raised from the dead. So the chief priests made plans to kill Lazarus as well, for on account of him many of the Jews were going over to Jesus and putting their faith in him" (John 12:9-11).

Hungry hearts are attracted to a life transformed by the Master. Lazarus was obviously an example of such a life. He was a shining witness of the love and power of God. Because of him, many were placing their faith in Christ. That honored God and helped others, but infuriated the pompous religious leaders of his day. What effect are our lives having on the culture and individuals in our society?

We've discussed two of the three gospel stories involving Jesus' friends from Bethany, now let's move on to the pivotal event in the saga of Mary, Martha, and Lazarus. This incident precedes the one from John 12 which we just discussed. John chapter 11 records it. It's one of the most momentous events in the ministry of Christ: the raising of Lazarus from the dead.

The drama begins with the statement of the simple fact that Lazarus was sick. His sisters sent a succinct but heartfelt message to Jesus, "Lord, the one you love is sick" (John 11:3b). Christ had left Jerusalem in the wake of an attempt on His life by His spiritual opponents among the Jews. He and His disciples had been spending the remainder of the winter on the other side of the Jordan

River, where many had come to believe in Him. Knowing how much Jesus cared about their brother, Mary and Martha likely expected Him to return promptly and heal Lazarus. It was not to be.

The Master's immediate reaction to the sisters' communication initially appears encouraging, yet is ultimately puzzling. "This sickness will not end in death. No, it is for God's glory so that God's Son may be glorified through it" (John 11:4). The implication to His disciples was that Lazarus was not going to die from this sickness. Nevertheless we know that the illness *did* lead to his death. And how are God and His Son glorified through someone's sickness? This statement by Jesus is just one example among many of Him speaking in what we might term "divine code." His disciples… those closest to Him… were often left scratching their heads at things He said, not grasping His meaning until much later. Why?

Fallen man is not inherently a spiritually sensitive creature. Our desire for knowledge of such things is usually weak. Even when such aspirations are stronger, our ability to grasp godly concepts is limited. Developing spiritual sensitivity takes time. It's a growing capacity which begins with seeking the face of God. In the closing days of His life Christ declared to His disciples: "I have much more to say to you, more than you can now bear" (John 16:12). He understood their limitations. It would take the ongoing work of the indwelling Holy Spirit to overcome their spiritual ineptitude. So it is with us as His followers today.

Through such challenging communications God plants seeds in our hearts that will only bear fruit after much time and care… watering, weeding, and cultivating. They stir passionate hunger and thirst within us. This yearning drives us to dig deeper into His Word and cry out to Him for greater comprehension of Who He is and how He works. As we pursue Him, a fuller measure of His grace is poured out on us. Remember the counsel of the Apostle Peter: "But grow in the grace and knowledge of our Lord and Savior Jesus Christ" (II Peter 3:18).

The next couple of verses from John chapter 11 raise yet another question. Verse 5 confirms Jesus' love for His dear friends. Verse 6 follows that up with a statement which once more evokes the query: why? "Yet when he heard that Lazarus was sick, he stayed where he was two more days." That this sentence begins with the word "yet" reveals that the inspired writer, who personally witnessed this scene, knew that Christ's action (*or inaction*) appeared to contradict His very real affection for Lazarus. If Jesus cared so much about the man, why did He delay going to his side to heal him. Why was He absent from what was a time of desperate need for Lazarus? The answers will come in due time.

When the 48 hours of postponement had passed, Jesus determined to return to the religious cauldron that Jerusalem had become, and deal with Lazarus' dilemma. "Let us go back to Judea" (John 11:7). His disciples again responded with consternation. "A short time ago the Jews tried to stone you, and yet you are going back there?" (John 11:8). The Teacher dealt with their bewilderment by speaking a riddle of sorts. "Are there not twelve hours of daylight? A man who walks by day will not stumble, for he sees by this world's light. It is when he walks by night that he stumbles, for he has no light" (John 11:9,10). He was alluding to the fact that His death could not occur until

SAM MASON

the divinely appointed time, but the twelve were probably mystified once more.

Christ then addressed Lazarus' present circumstances. "Our friend Lazarus has fallen asleep; but I am going there to wake him up" (John 11:11). As before, His words yet again brought more confusion than clarity. The disciples thought Jesus meant that their friend had literally fallen asleep, and took that as a positive sign of his impending recovery. This time the Lord corrected their misunderstanding. He had been using the word "sleep" metaphorically. "Lazarus is dead..." (John 11:14). Then Jesus went on to throw another monkey wrench into the mechanism of their human understanding. "...and for your sake I am glad I was not there, so that you may believe. But let us go to him" (John 11:15). Is there no end to the Lord's baffling words? Like His disciples of old, many times we ask that same question.

Troubled or not, they determined to follow Him wherever He went. The Master's hard sayings had caused some followers to desert Him in the past. On one particular occasion He asked the twelve if they also wanted to depart. Simon Peter's reaction spoke for the group. "Lord, to whom shall we go? You have the words of eternal life. We believe and know that you are the Holy One of God" (John 6:68,69). This time it was Thomas who spoke up. "Let us also go, that we may die with him" (John 11:16). Though at the moment of His crucifixion they would fall short of their aspirations, their heart's desire was to remain faithful to Jesus whatever the cost.

It had been supernaturally revealed to Christ that Lazarus was already dead, but upon His arrival in Bethany He learned that his friend had actually been in the tomb for four days (John 11:17). That would indicate that Lazarus had likely passed the very day that word of his sickness had reached Jesus on the other side of the Jordan. It's also apparent that the siblings were widely known and probably well-loved by others in the area, as many had gathered from nearby Jerusalem to comfort them.

When Martha found out that the Lord was on His way, she went out to meet Him. Though Scripture does not say why, Mary remained at home. Martha's first utterance in that moment exposed her sad and deep disappointment. "Lord, if you had been here, my brother would not have died" (John 11:21). All of the emotions which swirled inside her are not revealed in the account, but we can readily make intelligent deductions about what she may have felt.

Her expectation upon sending a messenger to Jesus was that He would come and Lazarus would be healed. Why had the timing of the Master's overall sojourn elsewhere led to her brother's death, and why had the Lord stayed away even longer after He'd received notification of their need? His absence in their time of crisis was mystifying. Martha was respectful enough not to accuse Him of callousness, or even ask the burning question "Why?" Still, her distress could not be hidden. She had anticipated the powerful intervention of Christ's Presence averting the tragedy which had now come to pass. The disturbing question pressed heavily upon her.

Martha's next statement demonstrated an abiding faith regardless of her disappointments. "But I know that even now God will give you whatever you ask" (John 11:22). Despite her grief, despite her earthly uncertainties, she was confident that the authority God had invested in Jesus was undiminished! Is that the kind of faith we have? Does our belief in the goodness and power of the Lord remain intact while our circumstances breed disorientation? Here's another question for us. Was there some specific expectation of what He might do now behind Martha's statement of faith, or was it simply a reaffirmation of her general trust in Christ? We're not told.

Clearly, though, Jesus *did* have a specific expectation in mind. "Your brother will rise again" (John 11:23). Martha misunderstood His declaration. In her mind, the present issue had been decided and any hope of her brother living and breathing again lay in the glorious future. "I know he will rise again in the resurrection at the last day" (John 11:24). The Son of God, however, was about to personify her doctrine. "I am the resurrection and the life. He who believes in me will live, even though he dies; and whoever lives and believes in me will never die. Do you believe this?" (John 11:25,26).

Once more the words of Christ created some initial confusion in the human mind. Two parts of His statement seemed contradictory. "He who believes in me will live, even though he dies..." and "whoever lives and believes in me will never die." Which is it? Will believers live *after they die*, or will they *never die*? Today we've come to understand that the first instance refers to physical death, while the second refers to spiritual death. The bodies of Christians will die and decay, but ultimately rise again. Our spirits will never die.

Martha didn't have the benefit of extensive New Testament study. She may not have fully grasped all the implications of His words, but she had no doubts about who He was. Besides being her friend, Jesus of Nazareth was the Christ, the Messiah, the "Anointed One." He was

God in flesh! In response to His query, "Do you believe this?", she unhesitatingly responded: "Yes, Lord, I believe that you are the Christ, the Son of God, who was to come into the world" (John 11:27). When we don't understand everything He says and does (or doesn't do), we can and should still trust in Who He is.

Having ended her brief exchange with Christ on a note of faith, Martha headed back home bearing a request from Him. Remember, Mary had stayed behind when Martha left to meet Jesus. Now Martha informed her sister: "The Teacher is here, and is asking for you" (John 11:28). Could it be that Martha's practical temperament had compelled her to greet her friend notwithstanding her painful disappointment, while Mary's more emotional side could not initially allow her to face Him in her great anguish? Whatever held her back at first was brushed aside in response to His appeal. "When Mary heard this, she got up quickly and went to him" (John 11:29).

Upon reaching Jesus, Mary fell at His feet. It's interesting to note that all three Gospel stories involving Mary and Jesus find her in the same posture: *at the feet of the Master.* Hers was clearly a heart of humble devotion to the Lord. We would do well to emulate her godly attitude.

As different as the sisters were in some ways, their approach to their brother's death was the same. Their first words to Jesus were identical. Like Martha, Mary asserted: "Lord, if you had been here, my brother would not have died" (John 11:32). Personal disillusionment saturated their thoughts and speech. The assertion that Lazarus was dead because Jesus was absent could easily have been translated into a four-word question: *Why weren't You here?* How many times might that question have been ours in the aftermath of some heartbreaking event in our lives?

The Lord was not indifferent to her pain. Witnessing her heart-wrenching sobs and the weeping of the Jewish mourners who had accompanied her, "...he was deeply moved and troubled" (John 11:33). Isaiah 53:3 describes the Messiah as "...a man of sorrows, and familiar with suffering." On many occasions Jesus had demonstrated His sensitivity to human hurt. Once more His heart was touched. "Where have you laid him?" (John 11:34) He inquired. They offered to take Him there. At that point the Master's feelings burst forth from his eyes of compassion. John 11:35 is commonly known as the shortest verse in the Bible. It simply states: "Jesus wept."

The Jews saw this as a demonstration of Christ's strong affection for Lazarus. They were convinced that Jesus deeply loved His dear friend. Still, like Mary and Martha, some of them wondered why He had not been with Lazarus, intervening in his time of great need. "Could not he who opened the eyes of the blind man have kept this man from dying?" (John 11:37). Again we hear the kind of question which has stirred at times in our own minds, and perhaps on an instance or two even slipped off our tongues.

Arriving at the tomb, Jesus was once more profoundly moved. This time though, He would release more than tears... supernatural power was about to surge from His being.

The tomb of Lazarus was a cave covered by a large stone. "Take away the stone," (John 11:39a) He instructed. Ever the practical thinker, Martha raised a concern. "But Lord, by this time there is a bad odor, for he has been there four days" (John 11:39b). She still did not comprehend what He had moments earlier told her about her brother rising again. We could not blame the Lord if there was frustration in His voice when He replied. "Did I not tell you that if you believed, you would see the glory of God?" (John 11:40). In obedience to Christ the stone was removed.

Looking toward the Throne of God, Jesus sent an intriguing prayer heavenward. "Father, I thank you that you have heard me. I knew that you always hear me, but I said this for the benefit of the people standing here, that they may believe that you sent me" (John 11:41,42). Two important facts stand out.

First, He spoke of His prayer in the past tense. Yes, He was praying now, but He'd previously spoken to the Father about the issue at hand and was confidently affirming that the matter had already been resolved in Heaven. This prayer was not a *request*, but a *declaration*. Christ had not been caught by surprise at the death of Lazarus, nor had the plan for raising His friend from the dead been a last minute impulse. Recall what He'd said to His disciples in John 11:11: "Our friend Lazarus has fallen asleep; but I am going there to wake him up." He knew that His Father always responded to His prayers, and He expected the miracle which was to follow.

Second, though His prayer was directed to the Father, it was offered *aloud* for the profit of those around Him: "... *that they may believe that you sent me.*" Again, let's look back to something Jesus had said earlier. "Lazarus is dead, and for your sake I am glad I was not there, so that you may believe." Remember, the disciples already believed that Jesus was the Messiah. Moments earlier Martha had also stated her faith in His identity as the Christ. While the unbelievers in the crowd needed an impartation of faith in Who sent Him and Who He was, those already following Him needed their faith strengthened and expanded. Not only was the man from Nazareth the promised Messiah, He had power over death. "I am the resurrection and the life" (John 11:25).

The next words Jesus spoke were not directed to the Father, or the crowd gathered around... they were aimed at the ears of a dead man! The Son of God raised His voice and raised the dead. "Lazarus, come out!" (John 11:43). Imagine the incredulous gasps of the mourners as the dead man, still wrapped in his grave clothes, hopped out of that cave! They'd never seen anything like this before in their lives. A man dead and buried for four days had been brought back to life! They had not simply heard the rumors, they had witnessed this astounding miracle themselves.

Christ told those in the crowd to take off Lazarus' grave clothes and release him. While they removed the death shroud from Lazarus, robes of another kind of death fell from the lives of others standing nearby. "Therefore many of the Jews who had come to visit Mary, and had seen what Jesus did, put there faith in him" (John 11:45). As *physical life* had been restored to Lazarus, *spiritual life* had sprung forth from those dead in their sin and unbelief.

Yes, Lazarus had died from his sickness while Mary and Martha wondered why Jesus was so far from them in their time of need. When He finally showed up in His own good time, however, something far greater than the healing of a sick man took place. He demonstrated His authority over death in an undeniable manner, and as a result many came to faith in the Lord. His absence had set the stage for a higher purpose than the healing of their brother... one beyond their most mystical dreams! While we lament the lack of God's Manifest Presence and the troubles which currently beset us, behind the scenes He's often preparing something special for us. How much do we really trust Him?

It's time to reach back and draw out some of the truths we've discovered in the three Bible stories of Jesus' friends: Mary, Martha, and Lazarus.

Lesson 1: Friendship with God Almighty is not an impossible dream, it's the objective of His plan for humanity. Open your heart and home to Jesus and you'll be opening a rich relationship with Him. The blessings of things like love, joy, peace and spiritual enlightenment will become yours. Pursue that friendship your whole life long. As it grows, the rewards will increase and deepen. Mary, Martha, and Lazarus experienced this.

Some people know something about God. We might say they have a divine acquaintance. They may attend church... perhaps even regularly. They might spend a little time reading a few passages from the Bible on occasion and send a "God help me, please" prayer heavenward in time of trouble. Sadly though, they don't entertain the Master on any regular basis. Don't settle for something so shallow. The Lord seeks more than a passing acquaintance with occasional small talk. He wants mutual commitment in an endearing long-term friendship with you!

Lesson 2: Service for the Lord is *good*, but intimate fellowship with Him is *better.* Martha was a diligent administrator and servant, yet she allowed the exercise of these divinely endowed gifts to rob her of intimate moments with Christ. Mary, on the other hand, sat at the feet of Jesus, soaking in His Presence and absorbing His wisdom. While we must serve the Lord productively, often through service to others, we cannot do so without spending adequate time in intimate fellowship with Him. The Word and prayer (listening to Him and speaking to Him) are indispensable. Truly effective Kingdom service must flow from close relationship with the King.

Lesson 3: Ministry to the Lord Himself can be costly, but God's commendation makes it worth it. Mary's sweet-smelling act of devotion to Jesus cost her a year's wages worth of perfume. It harkens back to King David's attitude in II Samuel chapter 24, when He intended to make a sacrifice to the Lord. A Jebusite named Araunah offered the king everything he needed for this act of devotion for free. David responded, "I will not sacrifice to the LORD my God burnt offerings that cost me nothing" (verse 24). It may be easy to surrender something *convenient* to God, but such acts have no depth of meaning. Let's be willing to pay the price when the situation requires it.

The cost of Mary's ministry to Jesus though, went beyond dollars and cents. She also paid the price of public reproach. In the eyes of some, her deed was deemed inappropriate at best, heartless at worst. Good intentions from a pure heart do not guarantee the appreciation of one's peers. Misunderstanding and rejection can be terribly painful. Yet the approbation of men is not the highest reward in life anyway. Mary's action received the stamp of approval from the Son of God Himself. Even when God's commendation goes unnoticed by those around, our real compensation will ultimately arrive. The greatest longing of every true servant of the Lord is to hear Him one day say: "Well done, good and faithful servant!"

Lesson 4: We don't always understand what God is doing or saying, but we can still trust in His goodness. The things Jesus said and did during the sickness and eventual death of Lazarus seemed puzzling. Our own life stories likewise sometimes produce doubt and confusion. Yet each new trial gives us another opportunity to trust His heart even while our heads may be spinning. And prayerfully meditating on His unfathomable words can help us grow in grace and the knowledge of Him and His ways. Don't give up, my friend, keep pressing on, for life in Christ is a growing experience.

Lesson 5: The Lord's apparent insensitivity to our circumstances is often actually His way of providing something better than what we might ask for or expect. Mary and Martha both greeted the Master with the misguided lament: "...if only you had been here." While we perceive only His seeming absenteeism, He's really working out a higher plan and purpose.

Walking with Jesus requires staying power during those shadowy periods when we wonder where God is. Hebrews 6:12 urges us "...to imitate those who through faith and patience inherit what has been promised." Like Mary and Martha, we need to learn that the lack of His Manifest Presence does not reflect divine disinterest. He knows what He's doing even when we don't. We must trust His loving nature and wait for His plans for us to be fulfilled. The Lord's ultimate purpose in a given situation may be revealed in this life, or it may not be grasped until we enter eternity. As Paul tells us in I Corinthians 13:12: "Now we see but a poor reflection as in a mirror; then we shall see face to face. Now I know in part; then I shall know fully, even as I am fully known."

CHAPTER 5

A CASE OF MISTAKEN
IDENTITY

We only know the name of one of them, but this pair are involved in a unique story. Their experience is documented beginning in Luke 24:13, but the preceding verses lay the foundation and provide the background. It was resurrection day. *Evidence* of this historic transformational event had been discovered, though *living proof* had not yet been revealed before these two headed out on their cheerless journey. The women had seen the empty tomb early that morning and were reminded by angels there that Jesus had promised to rise from the dead. Upon hearing their report, Peter ran to the tomb and found it empty, just as the women had said. No one, however, had yet actually seen the resurrected Christ.

"Now that same day two of them were going to a village called Emmaus, about seven miles from Jerusalem" (verse 13). Why had they left the other disciples behind, and why was Emmaus their destination? Scripture doesn't say. Could it be that knowing their beloved Master had been executed by the Roman Army caused them to feel they might now also be in danger, and thus they were fleeing for their lives? Maybe they had become so discouraged by His death that they'd given up on their Kingdom dreams and were headed home to Emmaus in utter defeat. Whatever initiated this unhappy trek, in God's design it would lead to a life-altering encounter they would never forget.

While these men trod the road to Emmaus "They were talking with each other about everything that had happened" (verse 14). As they discussed these events a stranger joined them... at least that's how they saw Him. It was actually their crucified and risen Lord who walked alongside the pair, "but they were kept from recognizing him" (verse 16). The difficulty did not stem from their need of new prescription spectacles, it was part of God's strategy for this moment. In a brief description of this same episode recorded in Mark chapter 16, the inspired Gospel writer noted that "...Jesus appeared *in a different form* to two of them while they were walking in the country" (verse 13).

This was not the first time the risen Christ had failed to be recognized by one of His followers. Earlier that very day Jesus had appeared and spoken to Mary Magdalene at the tomb. Initially she thought He was the gardener. Soon, however, her heart was filled with joy as she realized it was Him! You can read the full story in John 20:10-18. Sometimes such incidents occur because of our spiritual dullness. Still other occasions are the result of the Lord making use of divine teaching tools. Yes, God does disguise or hide Himself every so often. It's not because He wants to confuse us or play with our emotions. His glory and our good are always His primary objectives. Such was the case with the two disciples in this fascinating account.

This *stranger* inquired as to the topic of their conversation. "What are you discussing together as you walk along?" (verse 17a). It was not that Jesus was unaware of the subject of their deliberations. He was in fact there to correct their misunderstandings. God sometimes asks questions of His children, but not because He doesn't know what's going on. He not only knows our circumstances and actions, He hears our thoughts. His objective in asking us questions is higher than those of mere human beings. The Lord may be testing our honesty with Him, or He may simply be giving us an opportunity to pour out our hearts to Him. Ultimately though, our Heavenly Father queries us as a prelude to setting things right in our lives.

The initial response of these men to Jesus' question was not expressed in words, but in striking body language. "They stood still, their faces downcast" (verse 17b). The one named Cleopas broke the silence. "Are you only a visitor to Jerusalem and do not know the things that have happened there in these days?" (verse 18). At this moment Christ was not only a stranger to them, but also appeared to be a stranger to the crucial public events of the last few days in the Holy City. He seemed to invite them to illuminate Him. "'What things?' he asked." (verse 19).

Cleopas and his companion went on to update this uninformed visitor about all that had happened not only in the last few days, but during the last few years... things which had raised holy hopes, only to dash them in the end. They had seen the man from Nazareth as a powerful prophet, and even thought that He might actually be the Promised One, the Messiah. But their glorious expectations had come crashing down when the Jewish ruling class had not only rejected Jesus, but had had Him executed. The two travelers mourned the fact that this was now the third day since His crucifixion.

There had been some inexplicable occurrences surrounding the death and entombment of this prophet that very morning, but it seems they only served to produce more consternation. Some women had found His tomb empty and maintained that they had seen angels who proclaimed Jesus was alive. A few of His disciples had gone to the grave to find it empty just as the women had said. To their deep disappointment, however, no one had in point of fact seen Him. Grief and disillusionment continued to overwhelm them.

We might expect that the Master's first words following this tragic recounting would be encouraging ones. Not so. Instead His tongue danced with the powerful language of rebuke. Now, no one enjoys being reproved, but if we want to learn and grow it's a necessary part of the process. At times a gentle word of correction will suffice. Other times a figurative "slap up the side of the head" is required. Human beings can be notoriously thick-headed, especially when it comes to spiritual matters. The rude awakening that commenced would in due course bring these crestfallen men great joy.

Continuing His masquerade, Jesus spoke of Himself in the third person. "He said to them, 'How foolish you are, and how slow of heart to believe all that the prophets have spoken! Did not the Christ have to suffer these things and then enter his glory?'" (verses 25,26). It's not as if the disciples had never heard this before. On numerous occasions the Son of God had used the Old Testament to explain His mission and how it entailed His suffering and death. Yet somehow it just did not register with their spirits. It had not produced real faith. Though their egos likely smarted from His words in this moment, the rebuke was certainly in order. Plus in the long run it was for their benefit!

Thus began a most wonderful mobile Bible study. "And beginning with Moses and all the Prophets, he explained to them what was said in all the Scriptures concerning himself" (verse 27). I believe in the value of earthly teachers in the Body of Christ. I am called to be one. Understand though, they are no substitute for the Lord Himself. Every believer needs not only the ministry of Holy Spirit anointed teachers to grow in grace and knowledge of the Lord Jesus, but personal Bible study as well. Immersed privately in the Word of God, He Himself becomes our teacher, and there is none better! Cleopas and his friend were actually (though unwittingly) learning from the Master!

As they walked along, something not fully discernable began to stir within this pair. It hadn't quite risen to the level of consciousness, but it was stirring. Scripture passages they had heard and likely read before were coming alive with fresh meaning. A warm glow of light slowly began to break in upon their dark dungeon of doubt. Who was this stranger who had happened upon their path? The answer was uncertain, but the hopeful effect of His words was undeniable.

Time passed swiftly, and a once gloomy trip rapidly evolved into one of buoyant expectation. Almost before they realized it, they approached their destination. Or was Emmaus still their objective? As Jesus acted like He were going on without them, it seemed their destination was no longer a *place*, but a *person*. They didn't exactly know who He was, but they knew they wanted what He had been giving them. If Emmaus had been their home, perhaps they had now found a better one... a home for their heart.

Wasn't this why the original twelve disciples had left their homes behind to follow Jesus? When Christ called Simon Peter and his brother, Andrew, they immediately left their fishing nets to walk by His side. James and John did the same. Matthew (also known as Levi) abandoned his lucrative tax booth without hesitation to join the Master. Amazed at Jesus' supernatural knowledge, Nathanael (also known as Bartholomew) left his old life to join with the Man from Nazareth. This is the kind of impact the Lord had on hungry hearts.

In the aftermath of His crucifixion, His followers had forgotten the irresistible divine yearning that had in the beginning drawn them to a new kind of home... a *spiritual* home. Such feelings had fallen into the sleep of death even as the body of Jesus was consigned to a dark cave and sealed with a massive stone. That was about to change for these weary voyagers. Somehow this overwhelming desire had been aroused once more. Cleopas and his companion couldn't put their finger on exactly why, but for some reason they could not imagine allowing this stranger to leave them in this moment. "...they urged him strongly, 'Stay with us, for it is nearly evening; the day is almost over.' So he went in to stay with them" (verse 29).

Often God tests the intensity of our thirst for Him in a similar manner. Before He reveals Himself more fully to His people He wants us to demonstrate persistent pursuit of righteousness. One of my very favorite passages in all of Scripture is Matthew 5:6. "Blessed are those who hunger and thirst for righteousness, for they will be filled." We're inclined to think of the word "blessed" in such a pious religious context that we usually fail to recognize its broader implications. The Greek word for blessed, "makarios," simply means "happy." God is declaring that those who deeply desire His righteousness are *happy* people. Why? The promise declares why: "...for they *will be filled.*" A holy satisfaction of their spiritual appetite awaited these hungry disciples when they arrived at their destination.

We don't know where they were lodging in Emmaus. Was it a private home or a public inn? We're not told. We are, however, informed of a significant turn of events which occurred there. At the evening meal the *guest* became the *host*. When the food arrived at the table the Master took over. Jesus "...took bread, gave thanks, broke it and began to give it to them" (verse 30). The Son of God is a gentleman. He does not force His way into lives. He speaks the truth and stirs an appetite. Then He waits for a personal invitation. However, when the invitation is extended He subsequently enters our lives not as a stranger or even a guest. He comes as the Risen Lord of Life!

"Then their eyes were opened and they recognized him, and he disappeared from their sight" (verse 31). No longer was this amazing man a stranger, now they saw Him for who He really was: God in flesh! They had unknowingly been in the very Presence of the Lord. The patriarch Jacob had experienced a similar situation many centuries earlier at a place he subsequently named Bethel, or "House of God." He was fleeing his brother

Esau's murderous anger and found himself alone one night on the journey to his ancestral homeland... *at least he thought he was alone.* Awakening from an incredible encounter there with the Lord, Jacob thought to himself: "Surely the LORD is in this place, and *I was not aware of it*" (Genesis 28:16).

How many times have we too been in the company of the Almighty, yet failed to distinguish Him in the haze of disillusionment? Like the men on the road to Emmaus we may feel abandoned and discouraged, bewildered by our painful circumstances. Even as we begin to understand things and rise out of our pit of despair, our spiritual eyes are sometimes still blind to the One Who is right there by our side.

The means of this revelation is important to note. It occurred as Jesus "...took bread, gave thanks, broke it and began to give it to them." Why at that moment? What was the significance of that act?

First, the broken bread was symbolic of the Savior's body which was broken as the sacrifice for their sins and ours. The broken bread represented the body of the Risen Christ who sat before them. Their spirits suddenly saw the individual who had been brutally crucified by the Roman soldiers three days earlier... the leader whose lifeless body had been entombed in a cold dark cave... the person they presumed was dead and gone *forever.* They viewed Him now with eyes made new. This was the Bread of Heaven come down to be the Bread of Life here on earth. He was alive and with them!

I believe there is a second symbolism in the broken bread. It represents times of suffering here in our earthly existence. Frequently in the grip of suffering our spirits become more sensitive to the divine truths the Lord wants to impart. The mountaintop experiences of life may be more enjoyable than the valleys, but in the exuberance of those moments we spend in the rare atmosphere of emotional altitude, we tend to be more soulish than spiritual.

The trio of apostles on the Mount of Transfiguration with Christ had been more mystified than enlightened. One of them in particular reacted rather foolishly. "Peter said to Jesus, 'Rabbi, it is good for us to be here. Let us put up three shelters — one for you, one for Moses and one for Elijah.' (He did not know what to say, they were so frightened)" (Mark 9:5,6). Lest we think too badly of poor Simon Peter, we should remember that we've all said some pretty stupid things on occasion, perhaps even in the midst of a great event. I know I have. As much as we'd prefer to avoid suffering, it is often in those experiences that God reveals Himself to us in the most intimate of ways. So it was with Cleopas and his friend.

Jesus no sooner disclosed Who He really was to them, than he quickly disappeared. They would see Him again before too long, but for now they were left breathless at what had just happened. The stranger who had walked with them had been the very Son of God. Just as they recognized Him for Who He was, He vanished from their sight. Wonderment filled their hearts and minds. Their trek had taken them not simply from Jerusalem to Emmaus... they had gone from perplexed despair to enlightened jubilance!

This incident had bound the pair in a spiritual dimension they could never have previously imagined. There was now a deeper unity of faith that brought them together as one in the Lord. Their thoughts reflected each other's to the point where the very same question arose in both men. Scripture does not say that *just one of them queried the other on the matter*, it asserts that *each bounced the exact same question off his companion*: "They asked each other..." (verse 32a). Their amazing experience in the Presence of Christ had led to a shared contemplation which poured from their lips...

"Were not our hearts burning within us while he talked with us on the road and opened the Scriptures to us?" (verse 32b). It's not detectable in the above translation of this verse, yet these words in the Greek reflect further on the compelling unity which was the result of their unique encounter with Christ. A literal translation of the original text renders it as: "Was not the heart of us burning in us..." The key Greek word is in the *singular*, not the *plural*. It was not their *hearts* that burned, it was their *heart*. More than ever before they had become one in the Lord. That was the effect which the Presence of God had on this blessed brotherhood.

Now the men looked back on the road to Emmaus and recalled with awe how the Word of God formerly scribed on parchment, had been set on fire as it poured from the lips of the Word of God in flesh. What had beforehand been shrouded in clouds and mist had then flashed with the brilliance of the noonday sun. Their spiritual understanding had risen to new levels. Still, it was not until Jesus had broken the bread in front of them that they fully grasped Who He was, and realized the transformation His Presence had wrought in their *heart*.

The printed book with the words "Holy Bible" on the cover certainly transmits the true Word of the Living God.

It will never reverberate with its full effect, however, unless the Holy Spirit Himself speaks it to our inmost being. That may happen while spending time alone with the Lord, or while sitting under solid Bible teaching and preaching, but it will not come about unless the divine anointing rests upon it and us. Jesus had walked and talked with the two disheartened disciples. The fire that had dwindled to a few flickering embers within them was brought to full flame by the One who had first appeared as an unfamiliar stranger. Yet only in retrospect did they fully comprehend the glorious encounter that had taken place.

It should not surprise us that the Word of God is connected with fire in this story. The two primary benefits of fire are heat and light... benefits that also flow from God's Word. In a time of distress the Prophet Jeremiah tried to stop speaking the Word of the Lord. In Jeremiah 20:9 he explained the reason for his lack of success in halting his calling. "But if I say 'I will not mention him or speak any more in his name,' his word is in my heart like a fire, a fire shut up in my bones. I am weary of holding it in; indeed, I cannot."

The Psalmist recognized that God's Word would guide him through the dreariest of life's landscapes. He proclaimed: "Your word is a lamp to my feet and a light for my path" (Psalm 119:105). The fire of the Word of God shines brightly in a world cloaked in darkness. An encounter with holy fire can make the crucial difference in an existence growing cold and dark.

No one can sit still for long while a fire rages, and the fire Christ had kindled in them along the highway continued to blaze as these men now lodged in Emmaus. "They got up and returned at once to Jerusalem" (verse

33a). It mattered not to them that it was currently nightfall... the light within shone brightly. They were impelled to go back and tell the others the incredible news: Jesus was not dead as they supposed, He was alive and they had spent time in His rejuvenating Presence! When something this amazing happens to you, you can't contain it, you have to share it!

"There they found the Eleven and those with them, assembled together and saying, 'It is true! The Lord has risen and has appeared to Simon'" (verses 33b,34). The Gospels give no details regarding the Risen Christ's appearance to Peter, but the very fact that it happened speaks volumes about the forgiveness and restoration offered by our Savior. The bombastic Simon had declared that he would never deny his Master, but in fear and weakness he had. The One Whom he'd denied, first sent a reconciling angelic message back with the women who'd gone to the tomb. "...go, tell his disciples and *Peter*, 'He is going ahead of you into Galilee. There you will see him, just as he told you'" (Mark 16:7). At some point later Jesus made a special appearance to His broken and repentant fisherman/apostle.

Christ offers hope to all whose human flaws lead to doubt, fear, and even failure. Cleopas and his friend had responded to His crucifixion and burial with unbelief and despair. They fled from the scene of the crime. During the awful hours leading up to the murder of Jesus, Peter had claimed that he never knew the man from Galilee. Then in defeat and despondency he had gone out and wept bitterly. Yet all three of these men had been lovingly visited by the Lord whom they had let down. In the next forty days He would appear to many more, including "...more than five hundred of the brothers at the same time..." (I Corinthians 15:6).

Their outlook was changing from that of *hopeless mourners* to that of *hopeful messengers* of Good News. Such was the impact of the Manifest Presence of God, even after their frail spirits had initially failed to believe His promises, and their blurred vision had kept them from recognizing His personal visitations.

Now in the afterglow of a spiritual awakening, the family of faith shared stories with each other. Having heard of Simon Peter's audience with the living Christ, the pair who had recently arrived from their journey to and from Emmaus chimed in as well. "Then the two told what had happened on the way, and how Jesus was recognized by them when he broke the bread" (verse 35). Undoubtedly fresh praises to God filled the room as Cleopas and his companion reviewed their inspiring experience.

Thus the story of the two disciples on the road to Emmaus comes to an end, strictly speaking. But the verses that follow become an epilogue of sorts. They provide further comprehension of what happens at the juncture of the human condition and the Divine Presence. Let's comb that extended account for just a few more spiritual insights.

"While they were still talking about this, Jesus himself stood among them and said to them, 'Peace be with you'" (verse 36). This is the first incidence of Christ appearing to a *gathering* of His disciples after the resurrection. His greeting dealt with their need for calm in the midst of their present emotional turmoil, and anticipated the further bewilderment His sudden manifestation might rouse. Human beings are so often troubled, even during what should be wonderfully sacred events. In every circumstance of life we need the stability that the peace of God brings. The Prince of Peace, offered this vital blessing to His anxious followers in just such a moment.

In the accounts of His post-resurrection appearances in John's Gospel, the beloved apostle records Jesus saying "Peace be with you" *three* times. O how we need the peace of God! The Lord understands this better than we do. We're so naturally prone to fear and turmoil. No wonder He had to repeat the bequest over and over.

Despite His speaking peace to them, "They were frightened, thinking they saw a ghost" (verse 37). Again we're reminded of how spiritually dense we can be. This crowd had been discussing the proofs of the Living Christ some of them had personally experienced... yet when He actually emerged in front of them they were afraid, thinking He was a disembodied spirit! He had predicted His death and resurrection, He had subsequently revealed Himself to a number of them after His crucifixion and burial, now He appeared in the midst of the entire group. Still, they reacted with doubt and fear.

"He said to them, 'Why are you troubled, and why do doubts arise in your minds? Look at my hands and my feet. It is I myself! Touch me and see; a ghost does not have flesh and bones, as you see I have'" (verses 38,39). There are times when the Lord challenges us to step up a little higher. Other times He descends to our weakness. In this case it would seem He did both. He rebuked them for their doubts because He wanted them to raise their level of faith. Yet understanding their human infirmity He offered them visible and tangible proof that it was really

Him. Isn't that the way He'd just dealt with Cleopas and his fellow disciple a few hours earlier?

Even as Jesus showed them His nail-scarred hands and feet, they continued to distrust His words, and their own eyes. The reason for their qualms continuing at that moment is fascinating: "...they still did not believe it because of joy and amazement" (verse 41a). As we explained earlier in our brief discussion of the three apostles on the Mount of Transfiguration, emotional highs can interfere with both rationality and spirituality. The blundering reaction of this gathering of Christ's followers reminds me of the expression we might utter when something both pleasant and astonishing happens: "It's just too good to be true." We may pinch ourselves in an attempt to see if we're simply dreaming. It was not from disrespect of the Master that they doubted, it was because of "joy and amazement."

Christ continued to verify that He was *no ghost*. "'Do you have anything here to eat?' They gave him a piece of broiled fish, and he took it and ate it in their presence" (verses 41b-43). Again, the Teacher stooped to the limitations of His students. I love the earthiness of this occasion. He was indeed the Son of God come down from Heaven, but He was also the Son of Man born of a woman. Jesus ate in front of them to prove He was more than a *spirit*, He was some*body*. And I think He enjoyed every bite of that broiled fish!

During His earthly ministry Jesus had instructed His disciples *in advance* what the Scriptures had to say about His pending death and resurrection. Now, just as he had done with the pair on the road to Emmaus, He referred to those same Scriptures *in retrospect* as He spoke to all who had assembled there in Jerusalem. "This is what I told you while I was still with you: Everything must be fulfilled that is written about me in the Law of Moses, the prophets and the Psalms" (verse 44). Christ stood among them as flesh and bone proof of the veracity of those Old Testament prophecies.

The next thing the Lord did with this group is the flip side of what he had done shortly before with Cleopas and his friend. The two actions are clearly related. The traveling companions noted that while Jesus talked with them on the road, He "...opened the Scriptures to us" (verse 32). Verse 45 reveals that He did essentially the same with the crowd at Jerusalem. "Then he opened their minds so they could understand the Scriptures." In the first incident He opened the Scriptures to their minds. In the second He opened their minds to the Scriptures.

Either way you look at it, the work of the Lord in creating a synergy between our minds and His Word is vital to our walk with God. As we've noted repeatedly, human beings are slow to grasp divine truth. It's especially been that way since our fall into sin in the Garden of Eden. The power of the Lord, however, can overcome our spiritual stupor. The Resurrected Christ did it for His followers on this occasion, but He's no longer here in that form. In a few verses we'll see how provision has been made for those of us who live in this post-ascension world.

After opening their minds, He stated the essence of the Gospel as it was predicted in the Old Testament. "...This is what is written: the Christ will suffer and rise from the dead on the third day, and repentance and forgiveness of sins will be preached in his name to all nations, beginning at Jerusalem" (verse 46,47). Jesus then went on to declare their role in all this, and to reiterate the guarantee of supernatural ability from above which would enable them to be His messengers. "You are witnesses of these things. I am going to send you what my Father has promised; but stay in the city until you have been clothed with power from on high" (verses 47,48).

The Father's promise referenced in verse 48 had been introduced to the disciples by Jesus in John chapters 14 and 16. The first mention of it occurs in John 14:16,17: "And I will ask the Father, and he will give you another Counselor to be with you forever—the Spirit of truth." Christ was speaking, of course, of the Holy Spirit. The declaration that the Counselor will "…be with you forever" becomes an extension of a divine pledge originally stated in Deuteronomy 31:6,8, then reiterated in Hebrews 13:5: "Never will I leave you; never will I forsake you." This is the Covenant Presence of God, which is always with us, as opposed to the Manifest Presence, which is sometimes absent.

Jesus taught that as Counselor, the Holy Spirit "…will teach you all things and will remind you of everything I have said to you" (John 14:26). Remember a few paragraphs ago when I said that later we would see the provision God has made for opening our minds to the Scriptures since the Resurrected Christ (Who initially did that for His followers) is no longer on earth? The above quoted John 14:26 *is* that provision! John 16:13 makes it even clearer: "But when he, the Spirit of truth, comes, he will guide you into all truth."

We so desperately need our minds opened to the written Word of God! Whenever I open the Bible to study, I pray for the Holy Spirit to enlighten me to what it means.

That's the same kind of prayer the Psalmist offered. Particularly we find it in places like Psalm 119:125: "I am your servant; give me discernment that I may understand your statutes." He realized that he needed the truth that shines brightly in our hearts only when God's Word is brought to life by its Author. "The unfolding of your words gives light; it gives understanding to the simple" (Psalm 119:130).

The Spirit of God not only helps us to *understand* Scripture, He enables us to *proclaim* it effectively. Whether we're sharing our faith one on one with a single individual, or preaching or teaching to a crowd, we need divine empowerment. Whenever I communicate Bible truths I covet the anointing of the Holy Spirit. If He's not speaking through me my efforts lack authority. In Acts 1:8 Jesus promised this kind of power to those He would soon be leaving behind as He ascended into Heaven. "But you will receive power when the Holy Spirit comes on you; and you will be my witnesses in Jerusalem, and in all Judea and Samaria, and to the ends of the earth."

The brethren on the road to Emmaus had begun their journey in heartbreaking disappointment... maybe even with a sense of betrayal and abandonment. After all, they had reached out in faith to believe that Jesus of Nazareth could be the promised Messiah, only to have their hopes dashed. The One in Whom they had placed their trust was dead and gone!

Yet He was in actuality no longer dead... or gone. Though at first their eyes were blinded to His Presence, they eventually discovered that He was right there with them! They and their fellow disciples in Jerusalem were ultimately filled with joy and peace. They would soon also be filled with the Holy Spirit as they were transformed from inconsolable doubters into robust witnesses of the Living Lord.

So what are some of the lessons we've learned from the story of Cleopas and his friend? Let's look back...

Lesson 1: We all have moments when we're tempted to throw in the proverbial towel. The disciples in this story are no exceptions. They had obviously followed Jesus for a while, and had exercised some level of faith in Him. They had recognized Him as "a prophet, powerful in word and deed before God and the people" (verse 19). They had even dared to hope that He was the promised Messiah. But in spite of the fact that Christ had predicted His death, after He was crucified and buried, the faith and hope this pair had once exercised tumbled off the cliff of despair.

We might like to believe that our commitment to the Lord is strong enough that we're immune to that level of discouragement, but we're not. In His humanity even Jesus Himself suffered the assault of life's troubling questions. Hanging on the cross in excruciating pain, He felt so alone and abandoned that moments before He died He "...cried out in a loud voice 'My God, my God, why have you forsaken me?'" (Matthew 27:46).

The sin is not in experiencing negative emotions, it's in surrendering to those feelings. There will be times when the dark night of despondency envelopes you. Count on it. Just don't settle down and build your home there. Keep in mind, the darkest night is just before the dawn.

Lesson 2: During those periods when we think God is nowhere to be found, He may in fact be right there beside us. The men on the road to Emmaus were walking with the Savior even as they bemoaned His death and assumed His final departure. Though they didn't perceive it at the time, Jesus was their companion on that long, lonely journey. While they were unexplainably invigorated by His authoritative exposition of Scripture, they saw Him only as a mysterious stranger... *not* the Risen Lord of Glory.

Such numbness to His Presence can be the product of our own insensitivity. We could be walking in a stupor of emotional intoxication, spiritually anesthetized because we're wallowing in self-absorption. Let's face it, in the midst of painful circumstances it's easy to slide into the mire of self pity. There in that pit we tend to lose our usual awareness of anything or anyone else around us, *including the Lord.*

Or we may not recognize His Presence because God Himself has temporarily blinded us. He's with us, but He's not manifesting Himself. Be assured that when that happens He's not punishing us. It's part of the Lord's plans to teach us something in His unique way. Remember, His ways are not our ways (Isaiah 55:8). The things He does, however, are for the good of His children. That's His purpose. "'For I know the plans I have for you,' declares the Lord, 'plans to prosper you and not to harm you, plans to give you hope and a future'" (Jeremiah 29:11). Learn to trust His loving nature even when you can't see His face.

Lesson 3: Sometimes the road to recovery begins with a rebuke. Ouch! I know you didn't want to hear that again. Neither did I. I prefer comfort to confrontation. But if we're headed in the wrong direction we need an *about face.* Cleopas and his friend were on the wrong road, and I'm not simply talking about the highway to Emmaus. The road conditions included anxiety and hopelessness, and the sign read "The Old Life Straight Ahead." Somebody had to provide a rude awakening for these wanderers from the faith, and that Somebody was the Lord Himself!

Just as Jesus had to indict these men for "...How foolish and slow of heart to believe..." they were, so He must occasionally do the same for us. A 180 degree change of direction is not likely to come easily. Still, when God has to confront us in our error, the hurt we may endure is well worth it. We must identify it as an act of love. "My son, do not despise the LORD's discipline and do not resent his rebuke, because the LORD disciplines those he loves, as a father the son he delights in" (Proverbs 3:11,12).

Lesson 4: God is looking for those who won't be satisfied with just an occasional brief visit from Him. The traveling disciples had a taste of the Lord's resurrection life along the way, and they didn't want to say "see ya later" as He appeared to be moving on when they arrived at their original destination. They wanted more of what He had been feeding them, and so they urged Him to stay the night.

The Master will put our righteous desires to the test. If we want more of Him He'll work with us, but He won't force a greater measure of His precious intimacy upon us than we want. How do we signal our holy aspirations to Him? Once we've "...tasted the heavenly gift, shared in the Holy Spirit, and have tasted the goodness of the word of God and the powers of the coming age..." (Hebrews 6:4b,5) as these two did, we cling the more to Him. We study His Word, spend time in prayer and devotion, and come together in His Name with others who share our love for the Lord. There He's promised to be in our midst

(Matthew 18:20). We strive to live for Him 24/7, seeking to walk in the Spirit (Galatians 5:16,25).

Lesson 5: In the right time and through the right means, the Lord will reveal His Presence to us. The two characters in this account had spent hours in close personal proximity to the risen Christ, yet had not realized who He was. It was not until Jesus sat at the table and broke the bread that they suddenly recognized Him. We might like to choose how and when God works in our lives, but He is sovereign and He knows best.

As we mentioned earlier, the broken bread was symbolic of His broken body. The Lord often uses symbolism to awaken our comprehension of Him and His ways. When He does so, He's in a sense coming down to our human level of understanding. Jesus did that throughout His earthly ministry by using everyday illustrations as he taught. Now He had done it for this pair through the emblem of the broken bread.

However, I think that the broken bread represents even more than the Savior's own wounded physical being. It represents times of trouble in our own lives. Much as we may want to live in the constant euphoria of divine pleasure, there are depths of our relationship with God that can only be discovered in the midst of affliction. "We must go through many hardships to enter the kingdom of God..." (Acts 14:22). We must allow God to be God, and do things when and how He wills. Usually we can't fully appreciate what He's done in those difficult periods until we, like Cleopas and his brother in the Lord, look back and recognize how "our hearts burned within us while he talked with us on the road..."

Lesson 6: Even after God has mightily revealed Himself to us, we may still struggle with doubts. When the men returned from Emmaus and gathered with fellow believers in Jerusalem, the various reports of encounters with the risen Messiah reinforced their common faith. Then Jesus unexpectedly crashed their celebration even as they spoke. Their reaction to His appearance is surprising. Instead of receiving His Presence as an affirmation, they were alarmed and confused. What had happened to their recently renewed faith?

We'd like to think that once we have received such a remarkable divine revelation, spiritual uncertainties are forever gone. Not so. Fear gripped this band of disciples fiercely enough that the Lord had to breathe His peace into the room repeatedly. The struggle to understand the ways of the Lord and dispense with doubts continues to some degree throughout our Christian experience. Our journey is not one continuously exhilarating skip across scenic mountaintops. There will still be valleys too. Trust God to train you how to practice His peace during the periods of testing, and bring you step by step into a deeper walk of faith.

Lesson 7: The role that the illuminated Scriptures play in our spiritual growth can hardly be overstated. God has given all of us powers of intellect. Yet even at their best those powers cannot plumb the depths of God's Word. The pair from Emmaus and the group at Jerusalem had without exception fallen short in their grasp of Scripture. They needed the Master to open the Scriptures to them, and their minds to the Scriptures. Additionally, He had promised that after His ascension to Heaven the Holy

Spirit would be sent by the Father to carry on that crucial task.

Yes, the Lord uses earthly images to help us understand heavenly principles, but some truths cannot be fully absorbed without His direct intervention. The Bible was not inspired by mere humans and it cannot be wholly comprehended by mortal men either. On this side of eternity we must always look to God for His Holy Ghost anointing when we study the Bible. With His help we will learn and grow.

Maybe right now you too, are bewildered by what's going on in your life. Some deep disappointment has weighed you down, and in despondency you've wandered down a path to something you hope will bring a semblance of solace and stability. Could it be that on that highway God is actually beginning to expand your understanding and restore your faith? You're still struggling with discouragement… but something within is stirring. Like Cleopas and his companion, you may be temporarily blinded to the very Presence of the One Whose departure you mourn. Cling to your trust in the Lord even though you can't seem to glimpse Him. He's right there beside you, waiting for the right moment to manifest Himself. That Stranger Who whispers inscrutable sweet truths to your heart is Jesus Himself. It could be that on your part too, it's just a case of mistaken identity.

CONCLUSION

Chances are you've found your own personal experiences reflected in one or more of the Bible stories we've investigated. They may not exactly fit your circumstances, but at their core the essence is the same. In each case a child of God wondered where the Lord was. The truths derived from studying those accounts can help you understand and deal with your own difficult circumstances... even emerge from them in great victory!

It's possible that like Job of old, your trial in fact has its origins in the Lord's confidence in your godly character. Like the Psalmist our boast should always be in God (Psalm 34:2, 44:8). Still, it's wonderful to think that if we're faithful, *He may actually boast of us!* That's what He did when bringing up the subject of Job in a conversation with the Devil. How we respond to the enemy's subsequent attack can validate the Lord's positive assessment of us. Like Job, let's learn to trust God even in the grip of intense suffering. That will bring glory to His Name, and an ultimate reward to us.

Maybe the absence of the Holy Spirit in your life has come about in the same way as it did in Samson's. God has called you and endowed you with special gifts to use for His purposes. But you've taken it all for granted and allowed yourself to drift into sins of self indulgence. Your surrender to Satan in an area of weakness has opened the door for him to capture you and put you to work in his grinding mill. Thankfully we serve a merciful God who will restore us if we turn to Him in repentance. When Samson prayed, the powerful Presence of the Lord was restored to him, and the greatest triumph of his life followed.

Your path may parallel that of the ancient King of Judah. Hezekiah was a godly person and a noble leader of God's people. He honored the Lord and the Lord in turn honored him. Yet a spiritual malignancy was developing within him. Yahweh's blessings upon Hezekiah and his kingdom had come to be clutched as something he felt he deserved. God left him for a time to test him and help him discover this potentially deadly tumor that was in his heart. The temporary divine departure was for the king's benefit, bringing his attention to the problem. If Hezekiah's pride had been left to continue unabated, it could have destroyed his relationship with the Lord. The absence of God's Manifest Presence in your life might be meant to return you to humility and dependence upon Him.

Has tragedy struck you... tragedy which could have been avoided if only the Lord had responded to your pleas? Then draw encouragement from Mary and Martha's experience. They knew Jesus loved their brother, Lazarus, yet as illness sucked the life out of him, the Master was no where near their village of Bethany. The sisters never stopped loving Christ, but when He finally showed up days after their brother's death, they didn't hesitate to let Him know how deeply disappointed they were. Jesus' apparently untimely return however, brought something even better than Lazarus' healing. Their brother emerged from his tomb more full of life than ever before! God's absence in your time of need could be designed to fulfill a higher purpose to be discovered later in time or eternity!

Perhaps the incident involving Cleopas and his friend contain a message for you. Hopelessness dogs your steps as you attempt to make your escape from disappointment. The One in Whom you placed your greatest hopes seems to be gone. There is buzz among a few that He may actually be around somewhere... but they are after all, *only rumors*. Then you encounter someone or something strange on your journey. You sense a spark of hope, but the Presence of the Lord is still imperceptible. The spark becomes a flame as encouragement grows, yet it's not until God chooses to open your eyes that you realize He's been walking right beside you! Don't give in to despair, my friend. In His own way and on His own schedule He'll reveal Himself.

My hope and prayer is that through reading this book you've gained useful insights to help you through those periods when you see no evidence of God's active Presence in your life. If so, I want you to remember two things. Number one, these truths have not come from Sam Mason. They were solidly imbedded in the Word of God. I only helped you mine them and bring them out into the light. Number two, there may still be times when those jewels of wisdom will not seem to be enough for you. They provide *some* answers to your questions, but not *all*. Certain earthly riddles may have to wait until eternity for solutions. In such uncertain circumstances you'll have to learn to sustain your faith in the trustworthy nature of your Heavenly Father alone. You may not understand what

He's doing, but know that He's always loving, supremely wise, and fully sovereign.

Finally, my friend, look forward to the unmitigated joy that awaits you when this often troubled earthly life is finished. It's then that you'll experience the *Fullness* of your Heavenly Father's Presence. No longer will there be moments when you can't sense His dear companionship. Never again will you cry out: "If only I knew where to find Him!" You and I will by His grace be at home in His Presence for all eternity. Let the words the Apostle John heard coming from the throne of God as he glimpsed the Holy City, echo in your own spirit. "Now the dwelling of God is with men, and he will live with them. They will be his people, and God himself will be with them and be their God. He will wipe every tear from their eyes. There will be no more death or mourning or crying or pain, for the old order of things has passed away" (Revelation 21:3,4). When it comes to the blessings of His Presence, the best is yet to come!

Printed in the United States
By Bookmasters